TAIWAN

STUDIES IN CHINESE LOCAL HISTORY

Edited by Leonard H. D. Gordon

Columbia University Press
New York and London 1970

ISBN: 0-231-03376-1
Library of Congress Catalog Card Number: 78-108096
Printed in the United States of America

TAIWAN

STUDIES IN CHINESE LOCAL HISTORY

Occasional Papers of The East Asian Institute
of Columbia University

THE EAST ASIAN INSTITUTE OF COLUMBIA UNIVERSITY

The East Asian Institute of Columbia University was established in 1949 to prepare graduate students for careers dealing with East Asia and to aid research and publication on East Asia during the modern period. The faculty of the Institute are grateful to the Ford Foundation and the Rockefeller Foundation for their financial assistance.

CONTRIBUTORS

Leonard H. D. Gordon, Editor
Associate Professor of Chinese History
Purdue University

Harry J. Lamley
Associate Professor of History
University of Hawaii

Johanna M. Meskill
Associate Professor of History
The Herbert H. Lehman College of the City University
of New York

Edgar B. Wickberg
Professor of Chinese History
University of British Columbia

Contents

TAIWAN

STUDIES IN CHINESE LOCAL HISTORY

Introduction: Taiwan and Its Place in Chinese History

LEONARD H. D. GORDON

Among the provinces of China, Taiwan occupies a special position in that country's regional history distinguishing it from others. Since the beginning of the Ch'ing dynasty (1644), Taiwan has been a "frontier" area, occupied by mainland émigré and non-Chinese aborigines, as well as having been the object of foreign threat and seizure and the recipient of Ch'ing institutions. A major portion of the early history of Taiwan is one of seventeenth-century foreign pressure in search of commercial advantage. The story of the Dutch military and commercial establishment in southern Taiwan challenged by Spanish competition in the northern sector of the island is quite well known. Also, the heroic, and now near-legendary, efforts of Cheng Ch'eng-kung (Koxinga) to preserve the Ming dynasty in the latter portion of the seventeenth century are equally familiar to historians of China. It is the nineteenth-century history of Taiwan, particularly internal developments of the island, toward which a few western historians are now turning their attention. Between 1683 and 1887, Taiwan was administratively considered a portion of Fukien province and then briefly enjoyed provincial status until 1895. The historical problem being considered is the extent to which Ch'ing institutions had been developed during Manchu dominance of the mainland and the firmness of their hold on Taiwan during the declining years of the dynasty.

There are several reasons why Taiwan has been chosen as a province for special study in the field of Chinese local history. Some are reflective of a new approach to Taiwan, and some solely for reasons of expediency. First, the general interest in contemporary Taiwan, because of the political division between the Communist government on the China mainland and the National government limited to jurisdiction over the island, has stimulated a growing curiosity about its early history. China's claim to the island and political control over it, Taiwan's integration into the culture and institutions of the mainland, and earlier foreign interest in Taiwan are some of the questions being given attention.

Second, it cannot be overlooked that Taiwan is the only Chinese province now accessible to American scholars. The basic materials required for scholarly research, whether the researcher be historian, cultural anthropologist, economist, or a worker in some other field, are more readily available in Taiwan than in any other province.

Third, in the last approximately fifteen years, new documentary materials have been made available in abundance by Chinese historians on Taiwan. Under the auspices of the Bank of Taiwan (*Taiwan yin-hang*) and the Taiwan Provincial Documents Commission (*Taiwan-sheng wen-hsien wei-yüan-hui*), the historian has been given ready access to new material, augmented by the compilation of documents from older scattered works and the reproduction of local gazetteers. In addition to Chinese sources pertaining to the Ch'ing period, the studies and records made by the Japanese colonial government during the early period of its occupation have considerable value and relevance to developments in Ch'ing times (e.g.,

Edgar B. Wickberg's study on land tenure in northern Taiwan).

Fourth, Taiwan is small in size and has had a comparatively brief recorded history. It was apparently unknown to China before the eighth century, was not extensively settled by Chinese before the seventeenth, and was not closely governed before the nineteenth. Hence, Taiwan is relatively confined in both space and time, making it easier to study in its entirety.

Beyond practicality, Taiwan possesses some special features which make it different from most other provinces of China. First, it can be said that Taiwan, until at least the 1880s, had been a "frontier" region. It was comparatively undeveloped, an island detached from the core of China and occupied by a non-Chinese native population in the island's mountainous regions and the descendants of south Chinese emigrants residing along the western plain. While it can be said that all of China was at one time a frontier, its civilization having emanated from the Wei River valley in the north China plain, Taiwan is the last to have been developed in China's eastern regions. One problem of concern in all the papers that follow is the extent to which Chinese tradition—as it had developed and existed on the China mainland—was transferred to this frontier region of Taiwan.

A second aspect of Taiwan's distinctive character is that little political attention was given to the island while it maintained *fu* status in the province of Fukien. It was not until foreign pressures culminated in a French bombardment and blockade of Taiwan in the winter of 1884–1885 that the Chinese government felt compelled to take a more serious interest in the island, elevate it to the provincial level, appoint a capable governor (Liu Ming-ch'uan), and initiate an effective modernization program. Despite early Chinese aloofness, Ch'ing awareness of and feeling for the island were evident, belated though they were.

The papers that constitute this symposium are closely related in that they concern the history of Taiwan during the latter half of the nineteenth century, and they consider, among other questions, the degree to which Ch'ing institutions and traditions made an imprint on Taiwan society during the crucial and terminal years of Chinese jurisdiction there in imperial times. Moreover, they touch respectively upon social, political, economic, and international phases of Taiwan's nineteenth-century history.

In her discussion of one of Taiwan's most prominent families, the Lins, Johanna M. Meskill makes a sociohistorical study of a family being transformed from coarse and dubious origins to one of gentry status. Taking advantage of internal disorders, the Lins were able to increase their personal power and become an accepted member of the establishment. In her consideration of the period 1840 to 1895 Professor Meskill concludes that the "civilizing powers of the Confucian ethos" on Taiwan was effective to the end of the nineteenth century until Chinese rule was destroyed.

While many earlier writers have regarded the war of resistance against the Japanese occupation of Taiwan in 1895 as Chinese inspired and have attempted to show complicity between the Taiwan fighters and mainland leaders, Harry J. Lamley takes an opposing view. In his consideration of Taiwan's government, society, and defenses, as well as the leadership, support, and direction of the war of resistance, Professor Lamley concludes that the Ch'ing government did not wish to become involved in another war and that the clash in Taiwan was a "self-contained conflict distinct from the Sino-Japanese War that had preceded it." He compares it also with other local, limited, defensive actions by the Chinese against foreign military pressure in the nineteenth century.

Basing his study on Japanese statistics for the period 1898–1903 in three counties in northern Taiwan that are representative of the situation under Ch'ing rule, Edgar B. Wickberg has found that land tenure conditions were similar to the mainland in the rice-growing region of south China. Although land holdings were somewhat larger on Taiwan, tenancy and rates were about as high. Professor Wickberg also concludes that Ch'ing practices were maintained until the Japanese occupation of Taiwan.

In the final paper, Leonard H. D. Gordon considers the involvement of Taiwan in international power politics and concludes that the ability of the Ch'ing government to prevent the loss of Taiwan depended primarily upon the Co-operative Policy of the major powers, particularly Great Britain and the United States, to maintain the independence of Chinese territory. Once that policy ceased in 1895, the Ch'ing government was powerless to forestall foreign aggrandizement. Professor Gordon also notes that the Chinese unequivocally regarded Taiwan as a part of China and argued forcefully though ineffectively on traditional grounds that the island could not be severed from the Ch'ing state.

The first three papers in this symposium are revised versions of those presented at the annual meeting of the *American Historical Association* in New York City, December 28, 1966, and the last paper was presented at the annual meeting of the *Midwest Conference on Asian Affairs* in Kalamazoo, Michigan, November 1, 1968. I wish, as editor, to express appreciation for the encouragement and useful comments made by Professor Samuel C. Chu, Professor of Modern Chinese History at Ohio State University, at the American Historical Association meeting. We also wish to thank Professors James W. Morley and C. Martin Wilbur of the East Asian Institute of Columbia University for their encouragement and interest in this project.

The Lins of Wufeng: The Rise of a Taiwanese Gentry Family

JOHANNA MENZEL MESKILL

In the middle of the nineteenth century, the Ch'ing dynasty's power quickly eroded when serious rebellions broke out in several parts of the country, including Taiwan in 1862–1864. The resulting power vacuum was filled by regional satraps, a breed that has attracted historians interested in the phenomenon of "regionalism."[1] Less well known are other, more modest and strictly local usurpers of imperial power who arose in the wake of the dynasty's sharp decline. Yet the rise of such "overmighty subjects"[2] as the Lins of Wufeng undermined legitimate *local* government fully as much as the rise of a Li Hung-chang undercut dynastic power at the highest provincial and central levels.

While the emergence of "overmighty subjects" such as the Lins must have been common in many parts of

JOHANNA M. MESKILL is Associate Professor of History at the Herbert H. Lehman College of the City University of New York and is author of *Hitler and Japan: The Hollow Alliance* (1966) and editor of *Chinese Civil Service: Career Open to Talent?* (Heath series on "Problems in Asian Civilizations," 1963). Professor Meskill is currently working on a monographic study of the Lin family and their role in Taiwan's development from the 1750s to the 1890s.

China in the mid-nineteenth century, special conditions in Taiwan surely contributed to the opportunities they so successfully exploited. As a prefecture of Fukien province, Taiwan by the mid-nineteenth century was still a raw frontier area. In the western lowlands and foothills, where Chinese had settled, the population was lawless and turbulent, self-reliant in its conflict with the aborigines whom they had by now pushed into the eastern mountains, and defiant of governmental authority. Deep cleavages along ethnic and linguistic lines divided the settlers. Officialdom was unusually venal and indolent, spending a minimum of time in the primitive and malaria-ridden districts of Taiwan. Lacking effective government on the *hsien* level and engaged in chronic armed fighting among each other, the Taiwanese had created a whole series of illegal and semi-legal organizations for self-defense and self-assertion. Secret societies and private armed associations proliferated, as did "local bullies"[3] who lorded it over strings of villages from their heavily armed, bamboo-palisaded estates in the country.

In only a few cities in the western plains did the presence of a district magistrate and a fledgling gentry contribute to a recognizably Chinese pattern of stability. A few dedicated officials were beginning to contain if not to eliminate communal strife; and around Tainan, the prefectural capital in the southwest, a distinctly post-frontier society was emerging. But this slow "Confucianization" of the local power structure was severely strained during the mid-century crisis; now there arose unusual opportunities for men with a flair for direct action and an eye to their own advantage.

Such men abounded in the Lin family of Wufeng, a village about five miles south of the present Taichung, which did not then exist. Their ancestor had settled a century earlier in this turbulent area of mid-Taiwan; the family had been farmers and had by the 1840s attained modest wealth and local influence. The Lins were by no means gentry, no member of the family holding a degree or office. Rather, they were petty local strongmen, their strength resting on a privately organized military following and a network of kinsmen scattered over neighboring villages. The family's eldest male in the 1840s also held a small post as *pao-chia* head for a couple of villages but seems to have wielded at least as much private power as public. This, rather than any humanitarian succor of the downtrodden, probably explains the label "knight errant" bestowed on him by a famous Taiwanese historian of the twentieth century who was by then recalling the father of a line of heroes.[4] The man is important to our story only because of the manner of his death: in 1848 he was slain in a typical brawl with another local strongman from a neighboring village. Three years later his death was avenged by his eldest son, who despatched the killer on his father's grave, personally cutting out the villain's heart while invoking Heaven in the name of filial piety.[5]

It is the life of this twenty-three-year-old avenger, Lin Wen-ch'a, which forms the first half of this account. It was he who established the family's greatness. Wen-ch'a had notable assets for success in a period of political turmoil and violence. Personally brave and fierce in battle (years later, when a high officer, he still engaged in hand-to-hand combat[6]), Wen-ch'a had early shown scorn for an official career, abandoning literary studies and turning to dreams of military glory. Yet at the time of his father's death and revenge, he neither held a military post nor wielded enough private power to function as a local strongman. Despite intense local sentiment in favor of blood revenge,[7] Wen-ch'a had to submit to the local district magistrate's justice. Here he was kept confined, the regular death penalty, as so often, being set aside.[8]

In a pattern that was to become familiar later, Wen-ch'a's opportunity for freedom came in 1854. The island's military, beset by rebels along the northern coast, called on him to raise a force of braves and assist in the defense of the island. This mission accomplished, Wen-ch'a was given his freedom; he returned to Wufeng and relapsed into obscurity for the next five years. Yet these years were not wasted, for now Wen-ch'a built the basis for his spectacular military career of the 1860s. Still outside military officialdom, he strengthened his ties with the local military hierarchy by occasional donations of cash and provisions and by helping put down local disturbances. For merit or by purchase, he acquired military rank in 1858.[9] More important, he rebuilt the private power base his father had once commanded. By establishing a reputation for valor, distributing largesse, intervening in communal disputes, Wen-ch'a was able to gain a personal following. An unfriendly source may be referring to this period in the Lins' history:

> In the beginning, the Lin family was not so high and mighty. They were simply a typical big clan. It was at the time that [Wen-ch'a] became an official that the family began to be cursed.[10]

This turning point came in 1859 when Wen-ch'a, at the head of a contingent, the Taiwan braves (*T'ai-yung*) whom he had been asked to raise, crossed over to the mainland and helped the provincial authorities in Fukien and Chekiang provinces against local rebels and Taiping forces. His military successes on the mainland over the next few years became the basis for the family's rise to power in Taiwan, for the Lins knew well how to convert public office and merit into private power and wealth.

Lin Wen-ch'a's career contributed to the family's rise in a number of ways. In the first place, a series of rapid promotions came his way and carried him to the pinnacle of a military career. In 1863 he was made acting commander-in-chief of the Fukien land forces, a post that carried rank 1B. His victories brought him, in addition, many decorations and honorific titles, all of which, including assorted peacock feathers, are recorded in his biography in the *Ch'ing shih kao.* In Taiwan these promotions meant that the family was now ranked as *gentry,* entitled to all the privileges that went with that status.

Second, Wen-ch'a's exploits on the mainland permitted him to form close ties with high officials who would henceforth function as his and the family's patrons in Ch'ing officialdom. In fact, of course, his promotions would not have been so rapid had such patrons not provided him with opportunities for distinguished service and repeatedly suggested his name for honors and higher rank. From 1859 to mid-1863 the various governors and governors-general of Fukien and Chekiang furnished this vital support. When in mid-1863 Tso Tsung-t'ang became governor-general of Min-che, Wen-ch'a gravitated into the orbit of that statesman. Tso, who looked upon Wen-ch'a as one of his four top generals,[11] was to provide crucial assignments and honors.

Although these political connections helped his career and the family's fortunes, Wen-ch'a's rise was linked basically to his military performance. Through 1859 and a good part of 1860, Wen-ch'a fought in a secondary theater, battling local rebels in Fukien. From the winter of 1860-1861, his activities shifted to Chekiang where Li Hsiu-ch'eng, the Taiping *chung wang,* pressed a successful rebel effort climaxed by the conquest of Hangchow in December 1861. Lin Wen-ch'a helped in the defense of this vital area and, from early 1862 on, in Tso Tsung-t'ang's efforts to recapture this rich supply base from the Taipings. As one of Tso's top field generals, Wen-ch'a thus participated in one of the key efforts against the Taipings, one closely related to Li Hung-chang's Shanghai-based moves as well as to the siege of Nanking under Tseng Kuo-fan's over-all direction.[12] While successful in relatively important theaters of war, Wen-ch'a's merits remained strictly military; we do not hear of his undertaking the kinds of political and economic rehabilitation through which the great anti-Taiping leaders consolidated their military victories.

Throughout these years, Wen-ch'a's victories on the mainland remained closely tied to his power base in Taiwan. He depended on the Wufeng area for replacements of his core troops, a group of initially 2,000 braves, "dull in speech and sharp in battle."[13] He made use of relatives (his younger brother Wen-ming, an uncle, a cousin) to staff lower command positions, enabling these men to obtain regular military rank. Notably absent from Wen-ch'a's second-echelon commands were the local notables from mid-Taiwan, the kind of gentry leaders who in other provinces organized local corps (*min-t'uan*), indicating that Taiwan's gentry probably did not relish association with a military adventurer of the caliber of Lin Wen-ch'a.

The golden opportunity for Wen-ch'a to translate his official status directly into private advantage at home came in 1864. A rebellion in his native district, Changhua, had threatened both the public order and Wen-ch'a's power base since 1862. Several rebel leaders held private grudges against the increasingly domineering Lins, and rebels besieged Wufeng for more than a year, cutting off supplies and manpower on which Wen-ch'a depended. By mid-1862, within a few months of the rebellion's outbreak, Wen-ch'a's braves on the mainland were pictured as starving and unfit for battle. Yet it was only in the fall of 1863, on Tso Tsung-t'ang's recommendation, that Wen-ch'a's requests for reassignment were honored. He was now given a special imperial command to pacify the Taiwanese rebellion, his intimate knowledge of the area having recommended him to Tso.[14]

When Wen-ch'a returned to Taiwan in the winter of 1863-1864 the rebellion was already on the wane. Its limits had been exposed earlier when gentry-led local corps had confined the rebels to Changhua *hsien* and a few adjacent areas. Personal and communal divisions in the rebel camp were also beginning to tell. As a result, Wen-ch'a's troops played only a minor role in the recovery of Changhua city, concentrating instead on the pursuit and execution of the rebel leaders.

With the rebellion put down, Lin Wen-ch'a extended his stay in Taiwan and began to settle countless scores with old family foes. He had many of them condemned as rebels and confiscated their property, which soon came into the possession of his own family. A large town house in Changhua reportedly came into the family in this manner, as did hundreds of acres of paddy fields. Some land was probably sold to the Lins at bargain prices under the threat of expropriation. The chief addition to the Lins' landed wealth was the acreage south of Wufeng, which gave them access to the nearest large river and the irrigation system (*chün*) fed by this river on which the village had long depended. For decades this area had been under the control of the Hungs, a rival lineage to the south. During the siege of Wufeng the water supply had been cut off by the Hungs in an attempt to starve the Lins into submission. Under Wen-ch'a the Lins now took their revenge, stripping the rebel Hungs of their land and their water rights and incorporating them into the Lin domain.[15] As late as 1900 the rice lands of the Lins were still heavily concentrated in villages near Wufeng in which confiscation of rebel property had been pushed in the wake of the rebellion's defeat.[16]

The high-handed behavior of the commander-in-chief

and his kinsmen did not go unnoticed in higher places. Wen-ch'a and an uncle were impeached by the Taiwan intendant and the Fukien governor in mid-1864, whereupon the court instructed Tso Tsung-t'ang to investigate. Tso's report neither indicted nor exonerated Wen-ch'a but referred the charges to the Board of Civil appointments for proper action.[17] At this juncture Wen-ch'a quickly returned to the mainland, perhaps to plunge into further battles and gain fresh merits to offset these threatening developments. His services had been requested for some time already, and now that strong Taiping remnants erupted into Fukien in the fall of 1864, Wen-ch'a could not afford to procrastinate in Taiwan. The impeachment case still unsettled, he died a hero's death in battle near Chang-chou at the end of 1864. This settled his legal difficulties and enrolled him in the pantheon of Ch'ing heroes. Posthumous honors, including "Junior Guardian of the Heir Apparent" and seventh grade hereditary rank as well as honors for his ancestors, rained down on the fallen general, elevating the family to its pinnacle of worldly glory.

It soon became evident, however, that the Lins' eminence was precarious and that, without Wen-ch'a's military prowess and his personal ties to senior officials, they remained vulnerable on a number of counts. The uncle, for instance, who had been impeached with Wen-ch'a earlier and who now had the bad luck to escape from the battlefield where his nephew perished, was indicted for cowardice and put in prison for the rest of his life by the Fukien authorities. Wen-ch'a's younger brother, Wen-ming, a lieutenant colonel, and another uncle who also held military rank faced years of conflict with provincial authorities over disbandment pay for the Taiwan braves and charges of misappropriation of funds.[18]

While provincial officialdom had the means to call

the Lins to account, the district magistrate of Changhua did not. His authority, thoroughly undermined by the rebellion, would not revive as long as the Lins could with impunity take their neighbors' lands, houses, and women. Wen-ming did precisely that during the late 1860s, as we learn from several memorials of provincial governors who had occasion to investigate his conduct at a later date.[19]

If Lin Wen-ming, with his following of armed retainers, was beyond the arm of the law, a frame-up might still dispose of him. It was finally done in 1870 when some of the Lins' surviving enemies, the district magistrate, and others encompassed Wen-ming's murder in the *yamen* of the Changhua magistrate. The event has of course nourished local mythmaking, and it is difficult to get to the heart of the matter. Officialdom maintained that the execution of a dangerous disturber of the peace, on the spot and without benefit of trial, was legal; the Lin family tried for the next dozen years, though in the end unsuccessfully, to have the execution branded as murder and to have Wen-ming rehabilitated.

Under the circumstances, the family's resort to litigation rather than blood revenge may be viewed as a sign of changing times and of the emergence of new, less violent family leaders. Their special talents, patience and an ability to maneuver within the Ch'ing legal system, were needed if the family was to survive the decade of the 1870s, clearly a low point in their fortunes. Not only was the suit for Wen-ming's rehabilitation to be won, but the lawsuits of all the Lins' old enemies who now reared their heads and tried to recover their property had to be fended off. In the end the Lins settled for a favorable compromise. Wen-ming was not rehabilitated, but the family kept the lion's share of their spoils of the 1860s, their land, and their gentry status.

The rise of new leadership, particularly Wen-ch'a's son, Lin Ch'ao-tung, and a second cousin, Wen-ch'in, dominated family history in the 1880s and enabled the Lins to take advantage of the opportunities offered by a new era in Taiwan's history. Where Wen-ch'a had laid the basis for family wealth and might by exploiting the vacuum in local government and filling it with his own private power, the new generation made use of the return of dynastic power and stability to the island. In so doing, they raised the family from its precarious eminence to true gentry respectability.

The change in the local power structure to which the Lins skillfully adapted came in the wake of foreign threats to the island. The Japanese expedition of 1874 and the embroilment of Taiwan in the Sino-French war of 1884-1885 revealed to the dynasty its precarious hold over Taiwan. The previously neglected island now became an object of the court's solicitude; it was raised to the status of a province and given a vigorous governor in the person of Liu Ming-ch'uan. Liu soon began to promote not only some remarkable schemes for self-strengthening and industrial development but also the pacification and commercial development of the eastern mountain ranges, hitherto the realm of unconquered aborigines.[20] As Taiwan became more closely integrated into the Ch'ing state, it became necessary for the Lins to enhance family fortunes in close alliance with the newly strengthened provincial authorities, not against them as earlier. The new governor, in turn, needed the support of locally prominent families. This juncture allowed the new generation of astute Lin leaders to enhance their wealth and power while at the same time refurbishing the family's image.

The Lins had come favorably to Liu Ming-ch'uan's attention in 1884-1885 when they furnished braves and supplies for the defense of the island. Wen-ch'a's son,

Ch'ao-tung, maintained close relations with Liu during his entire tenure as governor, from 1886 to 1891. He held a number of offices under Liu, heading at one time the governor's military secretariat (*Ying wu ch'u*) and later the Bureau for Aborigine Pacification and Colonization (*Fu k'en chü*); he also led expeditions against the aborigines. In 1888 he quelled an uprising in Changhua district directed against Liu's attempt to resurvey the land and reform the land tax. Though ostensibly loyal to the governor, and rewarded on Liu's recommendation with the "Yellow Riding Jacket," Ch'ao-tung seems to have felt some sympathy for the rebels, if not their leaders.[21] In any case, he did not personally seize rebel land as his father had done after quelling a rebellion a quarter century earlier.

While Ch'ao-tung was a big figure in Taiwan's provincial government as well as locally in Changhua district,[22] his uncle Wen-ch'in, leader of the family's younger branch, stayed aloof from politics, devoting himself to business, local charities, and conspicuous filial piety. Both men built splendid mansions for their families, and Wen-ch'in in addition laid out the famous Lin garden, the *Lai-yuan*, in honor of his mother's eightieth birthday, recalling the name of one of the twenty-four exemplars of filial piety.

The economic base of the family was also changing in this last decade of Ch'ing rule, responding to new economic opportunities. Lin wealth, so far largely in land, became more diversified as the Lins branched out into the camphor business, the retail trade, urban real estate, and possibly coal mining in northern Taiwan.[23] Governor Liu gave Ch'ao-tung monopoly rights for camphor exploitation in the mountains of central Taiwan, and he was clearly the king of mid-Taiwan's lucrative camphor business by the early 1890s.[24] Wen-ch'in was also in the camphor business, maintaining his own firm with a permanent manager in Hongkong.

While the family's power grew and replenished itself along more legitimate channels, the real "Confucianization" of the family would have taken another generation under Chinese rule. Ch'ao-tung, the dominant personality from the 1880s on, lacked literary degrees, and Wen-ch'in's *chü-jen* status (1893) may have been purchased. A regular classical education under private tutors was the lot of only the younger generation, sons born around 1880 who, because of the sudden end of Ch'ing rule, did not follow this predestined route into Chinese officialdom. That the spirit of their Confucian education and devotion to public service was even then not entirely lost may be seen from the life of Lin Hsien-t'ang, Wen-ch'in's son and perhaps the first citizen of Taiwan during the half-century of Japanese rule, a leader of Taiwan's autonomy movement, a patron of culture, and a philanthropist.

Through the end of Ch'ing rule over the island, the Lins clearly remained "military" and "landlord" gentry, and never became scholar-gentry. In the somewhat pragmatic and anti-intellectual atmosphere of Taiwan where bravery and wealth counted far more than scholarly refinement, they were progressing well indeed. By the 1890s they were beginning to transcend the limitations of their purely military past. They patronized local civil *chin-shih* and followed traditional gentry pursuits in local leadership in flood control projects and philanthropy. Through such pursuits and through intermarriage, they now began to join forces with the older, less wealthy but more prestigious, gentry families of the island. At long last, even the strain between the Lins and the Changhua magistrate subsided, as both made common cause to advocate the site of present Taichung as the seat of the proposed new provincial capital.[25] Unquestionably, the Lins were among the handful of "first families" of the island when Ch'ing rule ended in 1895. They were clearly *the* most prominent family in mid-Taiwan, for some time the wealthiest and by now perhaps also the culturally most vital part of the island.[26]

The history of the Lins of Wufeng in this half-century illustrates how closely Taiwanese developments were linked to the larger trends of late nineteenth century China. The dynasty, hard-pressed by rebels at mid-century, fell back on the support of local gentry or loyalist "local bullies" to maintain its nominal authority. In the process, it bartered away many of the safeguards which had been set up over the centuries to protect dynastic power against bureaucratic factions and to shield local government from the incursions of "overmighty subjects." The whole structure of the "rules of avoidance" came crashing down as officials like Tseng Kuo-fan and Li Hung-chang built their bureaucratic machines within the scaffolding of the imperial government, and as men like Lin Wen-ch'a undercut regular local government on the strength of a special imperial command.

At the same time, the second half of this account shows that some life was still left in the Ch'ing state, which in the decade before 1895 gave the island more orderly government than it had ever known. We also recognize the perennial hold of traditional values over the self-made strong men of a Chinese frontier region. The transformation from local strongman to local gentry might well have taken a bit longer for an ambitious family in a mainland province. There is, however, little doubt that the Lin story illustrates an old theme in Chinese social history, the recruitment of a respectable elite from dubious antecedents that testifies to the civilizing powers of the Confucian ethos until the very end of the nineteenth century.

Notes

1. See especially Franz Michael, "Military Organization and Power Structure of China during the Taiping Rebellion," *Pacific Historical Review*, XVIII (1949), 469-83, and Stanley Spector, *Li Hung-chang and the Huai Army* (Seattle, 1964), including Michael's preface.

2. J. H. Hexter, "A New Framework for Social History," in *Reappraisals in History* (New York, 1961).

3. This is the modern translation, used among others by Mao Tse-tung, of an old Chinese term, *t'u-hao*, which has been used traditionally for individuals or families of local wealth and power. Whether the implication of the English term "bully" has always been present is unclear.

4. Lien Heng, *T'ai-wan t'ung-shih* (Taipei, 1962), p. 894. This edition, as others cited below, belongs to the very useful series "T'ai-wan Wen-hsien Ts'ung-k'an," edited by the economic research division of the Taiwan bank.

5. Lin Hsien-t'ang, ed., *Hsi-ho Lin-shih tsu-p'u* (Taichung, 1935), biography of Lin Wen-ch'a.

6. Takatori Taichiro, *Rin Bun-satsu den* (Taichung?, 1919?), p. 14.

7. Illustrated by Lien Heng's attitude toward a case of blood revenge, *T'ai-wan t'ung-shih*, p. 1003.

8. On the government's flexible position in Ch'ing times, see T'ung-tsu Ch'ü, *Law and Society in Traditional China* (Paris, 1961), pp. 82-87.

9. There is some disagreement among the sources about the timing and mode of many of his promotions. Family-sponsored sources often put the promotion earlier than official

sources, and allege merit rather than purchase. In 1858, Wen-ch'a acquired the rank of major.

10. Li Hsien-chang, "Shou Chih Kung-t'ang," *T'ai-wan min-chien wen-hsüeh Chi* (Taipei, 1935).

11. Tso Tsung-t'ang, *Tso Wen-hsiang kung tsou-tu* (Taipei, 1960), p. 2, a memorial dated T'ung-chih [TC] 2/4/28.

12. For a discussion of loyalist and Taiping strategies at this stage of the rebellion, see Franz Michael, *The Taiping Rebellion I* (Seattle, 1966), especially pp. 166-67.

13. Lien Heng, *T'ai-wan t'ung-shih,* p. 894.

14. Tso Tsung-t'ang, *Tso Wen-hsiang kung tsou-tu,* p. 4, memorial of TC 2/7/28. After its leader, the rebellion in Taiwan is known as the Tai Wan-sheng rebellion.

15. Interview with a staff member of the *Ts'ao-t'un shui-li-hui,* the public agency which now coordinates the local irrigation resources and preserves historical records concerning their development.

16. This conclusion emerges from a study of place names in Li, *T'ai-wan Min-chien wen-hsüeh Chi,* and in the land register books (*Shen kao-shu*) of Wufeng and environs.

17. Summary of the impeachment and the court order to Tso in *Ch'ing mu-tsung shih-lu hsüan-chi* (Taipei, 1964), TC 3/7/18. For details, see the impeaching intendant Ting Yüeh-chien's *Chih-t'ai pi-kao-lu* (Taipei, 1959), pp. 462-72, 580-85. Tso's investigation report is summarized in Wen-ch'a's biography in *Ch'ing-shih Lieh-chuan* (Shanghai, 1928), 51/9a.

18. See biographies of Lin Tien-kuo and Lin Wen-feng in *Hsi-ho Lin-shih tsu-p'u.*

19. These memorials are part of the litigation arising out of Wen-ming's death and are recorded in *Ch'ing mu-tsung shih-lu hsüan-chi,* TC 9/5/6 and 10/9/9; and in Ch'ing te-tsung shih-lu hsüan-chi (Taipei, 1964), Kuang-hsü, 4/12/26 and 8/6/21.

20. See Samuel C. Chu, "Liu Ming-ch'uan and the Modernization of Taiwan," *Journal of Asian Studies,* XXIII (1963/1964), 37–53.

21. Ch'ao-tung's biography in *Hsi-ho lin-shih tsu-p'u.*

22. Remarks by Liu Ming-ch-uan to that effect are cited in Harry J. Lamley's "The Taiwan Literati and Early Japanese Rule" (University of Washington, doctoral dissertation, 1964), p. 120.

23. Information provided by family members and former associates of a Lin-owned retail store in Tali. Coal mining by Ch'ao-tung is mentioned in A. B. Woodside, "T'ang Ching-sung and the Rise of the 1895 Taiwan Republic," *Papers on China,* XVII, 165, where Ch'ao-tung's role in the cession crisis receives some attention.

24. A. Mitchell, *Camphor in Japan and Formosa* (London, 1900), p. 52, and Ch'ao-tung's biography in *Hsi-ho lin-shih tsu-p'u.*

25 Takatori, *Rin Bun-satsu den,* p. 25.

26. On this point see Lamley, "The Taiwan Literati and Early Japanese Rule," p. 100, quoting Liu Ming-ch'uan.

Glossary

Wufeng	霧峯
Lin Wen-ch'a	林文察
T'ai-yung	台勇
Li Hsiu-ch'eng	李秀成
chung wang	忠王
min-t'uan	民團
Lin Wen-ming	林文明
Changhua	彰化
chün	圳
Lin Ch'ao-tung	林朝棟
Lin Wen-ch'in	林文欽
Ying Wu Ch'u	營務處
Fu K'en Chü	撫墾局
Lai-yüan	萊園
t'u-hao	土豪
Shen Kao-shu	申告書
Tai Wan-sheng	戴萬生
Lin Hsien-t'ang	林獻堂

The 1895 Taiwan War of Resistance: Local Chinese Efforts against a Foreign Power

HARRY J. LAMLEY

As an aftermath of the first Sino-Japanese War of 1894-1895, China was forced to cede Taiwan and the nearby Pescadores islands to Japan. The Japanese had already, during the war, seized the Pescadores quite easily. The occupation of Taiwan following the peace settlement, however, proved to be a much more arduous undertaking. Hostilities broke out immediately after Japanese occupation troops made their initial landings there on May 29, 1895. Although these forces gained possession of the capital (Taipei) and most of the rest of northern Taiwan within ten days' time, the Japanese subsequently were drawn into a prolonged struggle with local resistance units in other portions of the island to the south. Altogether, almost five months were required before Japan was able to secure control over the more densely settled lowland areas of Taiwan and bring such organized resistance to an end.

HARRY J. LAMLEY is Associate Professor of History at the University of Hawaii. His special field of research interest is the history of Taiwan on which he is currently preparing a monographic study. He has published "The 1895 Taiwan Republic: A Significant Episode in Modern Chinese History," *The Journal of Asian Studies,* XXVII, 4 (August, 1968), pp. 739-62.

The 1895 Taiwan War of Resistance

This five-month struggle is treated in this study as a self-contained war distinct from the Sino-Japanese War, which had terminated with the signing of the Treaty of Shimonoseki in April.[1] Once again Chinese were pitted against Japanese forces, but this time the fighting was confined solely to the terrain of Taiwan. Moreover, no direct confrontation between the Ch'ing and Meiji governments transpired. By the time hostilities broke out in Taiwan the Ch'ing court seemed quite willing to part with the island, if only Japan could be placated and made to restore the Liaotung Peninsula to China. In mid-May the court had issued instructions stating that no more troops and supplies were to be sent to Taiwan from ports in China.[2] Then, on May 20, an imperial edict ordered that all civil and military authorities on the island be sent back to the mainland.[3] Finally, on June 2, in accordance with the cession terms of the peace treaty, a Chinese commissioner, representing the Ch'ing government, formally turned Taiwan over to Japan amid ceremonies conducted on shipboard off the island port of Keelung.[4] At this point China officially relieved herself of all further responsibility for the affairs of her former island province, and the struggle for Taiwan, which had commenced five days previously, remained a separate, undeclared war.

The Japanese refused to admit that the occupation of Taiwan had embroiled their nation in another war. Instead, they steadfastly maintained that their military operations on the island merely constituted a mop-up of what they termed "local brigands and insurgents" (*doki sōzoku*).[5] However, this stock phrase, used against those accused of fomenting civil strife or rebellion, was not an apt description of the overall resistance their troops encountered in Taiwan during 1895. These occupation forces faced a predominantly Chinese population which had not yet acknowledged Japanese sovereignty over their island homeland. Moreover, the resistance they met stemmed largely from defenders who wished to protect their localities and save Taiwan for China rather than lawless elements intent on pillaging or seizing power. What the Japanese had mainly to overcome during their five-month struggle for Taiwan was a series of defensive buildups organized by patriotic resistance leaders who worked within the existing local Chinese administrative framework established under Ch'ing rule.

This study focuses on the local conditions and events in Taiwan during 1895, so that the sustained resistance encountered by the Japanese may be better understood. Brief accounts of the setting and nature of the war, the leadership and organization behind the main resistance efforts, as well as each phase of the conflict are presented below. From the general picture that emerges, a separate war marking a critical juncture in Taiwan's past comes to light—one corresponding to other limited wars which China waged against various foreign powers during the nineteenth century. As the final section of this study endeavors to show, the Taiwan war of resistance proved, in effect, to be one more such localized conflict in which Chinese defenders attempted unsuccessfully to withstand better trained and equipped military forces of a foreign power.

THE SETTING AND GENERAL NATURE OF THE WAR

The setting of the war of resistance is important to note, for by 1895 Taiwan was no longer the raw frontier it had once been earlier in the Ch'ing period. The local Chinese inhabitants numbered well over two and a half million, and their main areas of settlement had come to resemble southern Fukien and eastern Kwangtung communities across the Taiwan Strait on the mainland. Moreover, the Ch'ing government belatedly had adopted more positive policies to settle the island and develop its resources following the brief appearance of a Japanese military expedition there in 1874. The seven years Liu Ming-ch'uan presided over the government of Taiwan witnessed the most rapid implementation of such policies. The fact that Taiwan was elevated to provincial status as China's first and only island province several years after Liu's arrival in 1884 suggests the impressive advances made there during the latter part of the nineteenth century. From both a political and socio-cultural standpoint, Taiwan was rapidly becoming an integral part of South China.[6]

Taiwan's transition from a raw frontier area during the Ch'ing period had not been a peaceful one. From the late seventeenth century to the latter part of the nineteenth, uprisings were frequent on the island; and from the time of the Opium War, the possibility of foreign attack seemed an ever present danger. Faced with the problem of guarding against armed assaults of both an external and internal nature, the Ch'ing authorities gradually devised stronger defenses for Taiwan during the nineteenth century. In the 1860s local officials began encouraging members of the island gentry to organize and train militia units.[7] Then, following the brief appearance of the Japanese military expedition in 1874, more modern-type military battalions were sent to Taiwan to supplement the ineffective Green Standard forces stationed there.[8] The combination of these new battalions and local militia units paid off in 1884-1885, when Liu Ming-ch'uan made effective use of such troops to ward off a protracted French attack on the northern portion of the island. Later on, as the first governor of Taiwan, Liu carried out a number of reforms that bolstered the island's defenses.[9] Although many of Liu's reforms were allowed to lag after he departed in 1891, his self-strengthening policies were partly accepted in 1894, when military preparations against a possible Japanese attack were initiated. Subsequently, his achievements had a direct bearing on the manner in which the defenses were planned and resistance carried out on the island during 1895, particularly in northern Taiwan.

Such factors as the elaborate defense preparations, the aroused Chinese population, and Taiwan's long background of armed strife made it almost inevitable that localized warfare of some sort would break out in Taiwan whenever Japanese forces arrived to occupy the island. In 1895 the activities of key resistance leaders, together with the appearance of the short-lived Taiwan Republic late in May, gave impetus to the agitation for war on the island. Soon thereafter, a prolonged struggle did materialize during the Japanese take-over.

From the more reliable accounts one may conclude that this five-month conflict featured the usual grim hardships and suffering of warfare, yet yielded little glory for either side. The number of armed participants was quite large considering the relatively narrow coastal and hill areas of the island where the action was mainly concentrated. In all, the Japanese occupation forces consisted of two and a half divisions totaling some 50,000 troops. These forces were accompanied by about 26,000 "coolies" from Japan and at times were supported by Japanese naval units.[10] The local defense forces active in the different phases of the war totaled well over 100,000 Chinese combatants hailing from both the mainland and various Taiwan localities. These included Hsiang, Huai and Ch'u battalions, troops from Fukien, Black Flag and volunteer units from Kwangtung, and a diverse assortment of local Taiwan forces.[11]

Altogether, the mortality count of the war was fairly high. The Japanese may have lost as many as 7,000 troops, largely through disease. The losses incurred by the defenders due to battle casualties and epidemics undoubtedly were much greater. Even though few large-scale battles were fought, fatalities from sickness and infections contracted during the war made the casualty figures soar on both sides.[12]

Untold numbers of noncombatants in Taiwan also suffered heavily throughout the war. Epidemics of cholera and typhus raged among the populace of war-torn localities as well as the fighting forces of both sides. Again, the Japanese civilian newcomers to the island, officials and coolies alike, were afflicted by endemic diseases, particularly malaria. As the war extended into the autumn months, Chinese inhabitants of the central and southern districts of Taiwan also experienced floods, and soon thereafter famine in some areas, resulting in casualties among the local population. Moreover, numerous inhabitants were wounded and killed whenever fighting broke out in urban areas, as during the battles for the walled towns of Chang-hua and Chia-i. Rural dwellers met similar fates when Japanese units attacked and at times razed whole villages in order to disperse local resistance forces in the line of march or quell partisan bands operating in rear areas already under military occupation.[13] Meanwhile, nearly the entire local Chinese population of Taiwan experienced hardships and uncertainties related to the cession of their island homeland. Even before the Sino-Japanese War ended in April, rumors to the effect that Japan would seize Taiwan created adverse conditions there. Noticeable signs of unrest became evident late in March, when a small Japanese expeditionary force took possession of the Pescadores. By the end of the month, as news spread that an armistice applicable only to North

China had been arranged, panic broke out in Taiwan. Ch'ing officials and their dependents began to depart for the mainland, as did members of wealthy merchant and gentry families. Local order commenced to break down and, as one witness described it, "bandits rose up like hair" about the island.[14]

For approximately the next two months, the Chinese inhabitants experienced great anxiety. After reports of the cession of Taiwan had been confirmed, the general impression that both they and their island homeland had been abandoned by the Ch'ing court became prevalent. Near anarchy prevailed in many areas where disreputable local elements and disgruntled military units commenced to take matters into their own hands. During the latter part of April, salt and likin offices at I-lan, Chang-hua, and other districts were sacked. In Taipei even the governor's *yamen* was attacked by a mob. Throughout northern Taiwan the situation remained especially tense as more ill-trained and undisciplined Kwangtung troops continued to arrive from the mainland.[15]

Such chaotic conditions ultimately had an adverse effect on the resistance efforts against the Japanese. Local leaders were unable to utilize fully the available manpower and resources on the island. Only a minority of the inhabitants actively supported the defensive operations in their areas. The majority stayed in seclusion while several thousand others, who managed to secure passage to the mainland, made hasty departures from the island bearing with them what wealth they could carry.[16] During the war the matter of self-survival seems to have been the main preoccupation of most local groups. Oftentimes both villagers and townspeople tried to appease whichever side happened to occupy or pass through their vicinities.[17] Otherwise, banditry and unruly neighborhood elements remained among their chief concerns.

Strife among the inhabitants themselves grew more serious in 1895, as the tense situation tended to deepen the long existing cleavages among Taiwan's diverse social groups. The Chinese who experienced turmoil in their own localities became more fearful of attacks by the dreaded indigenous tribesmen of nearby mountainous areas. Again, the Chinese inhabitants of Fukienese ancestry, the Hoklos, were alarmed over the arms and training then being received by their habitual foes and rivals, the local Hakkas. In addition, the Chinese populace, Hoklos and Hakkas alike, came to resent the presence of turbulent mainland troops stationed about the island.[18]

Such adversities and tensions lasted on the local scene throughout the entire war period. The long expected arrival of the Japanese, known at first only as fearsome "dwarf bandits" to most inhabitants, merely compounded the panic and turmoil in Taiwan. The Japanese, in turn, were troubled by bandit groups and local disturbances in areas they occupied, just as were the resistance forces in the unoccupied portions of the island. During the war the Japanese depended on collaborators in some localities to aid them in restoring order and hunting down troublesome outlaw elements.[19] Meanwhile, two of the most bloody battles fought by local Chinese units were not encounters with the Japanese, but rather actions taken against marauding Kwangtung troops near the town of Hsin-chu and, later on, belligerent Hakka villagers in the Tainan prefecture.[20]

In all, the war and its background tended to cause conditions in Taiwan to regress to the point where fundamental social and political problems that had beset the island for over two centuries under Ch'ing rule again became acute. Turbulent conditions, portrayed by the old adage, "an uprising every three years, a rebellion every five," set in once more. In addition, the need of stronger and more centralized government on the island re-emerged as a crucial issue. As late as 1885, when Taiwan had come under French attack, this lack had been apparent. Then the rivalry between the Taiwan intendant in the south and Liu Ming-ch'uan, who commanded the defenses in the north, had jeopardized the security of the island.[21] During 1895, as will be shown below, rival leaders appeared in three main centers of resistance, instead of two as during the French war.

Furthermore, despite the fact that Taiwan had recently been made a province, an island-wide provincial outlook on the part of most inhabitants had not yet formed to compensate for their disparate social groupings. The 1895 war served to retard such a development. Even among those inhabitants who did volunteer to bear arms at one time or another during the war, most exhibited more interest in protecting their own home areas than in defending the island as a whole against the Japanese. Their attitude is not surprising among such a disturbed and suffering populace already so diverse in background and localized in outlook.

THREE MAIN RESISTANCE LEADERS

Under such circumstances, it is rather remarkable that a sustained defensive war was able to be waged against the Japanese occupation forces in 1895. This feat was made possible, in part, by the actions of resistance leaders who both before and during the war were able to take advantage of the prevailing political and social conditions and devise defenses for portions of the island. Three such leaders, T'ang Ching-sung, Ch'iu Feng-chia, and Liu Yung-fu, have been credited as outstanding contributors to Taiwan's resistance efforts, although eventually all three elected to cross over to the mainland rather than face the enemy when Japanese forces loomed close at hand in their respective areas.

T'ang Ching-sung, in his capacity as acting governor and for a time president of the Taiwan Republic, remained the foremost resistance leader on the island prior to his hasty departure from Taipei on June 5.[22] The nature of the defenses of Taiwan and the deployment of military units in the northern portion of the island at the start of the war reflect his influence while governor and president. Previous to his appointment as governor, T'ang had served as provincial treasurer of Taiwan. In this capacity he shared in the defense preparations begun under the timorous governor, Shao Yu-lien. However, T'ang's influence over military affairs had been overshadowed by several mainland authorities, including the Fukien admiral, Yang Ch'i-chen, and the renowned Black Flag leader, Liu Yung-fu, who were sent to the island shortly before war between China and Japan was declared in August, 1894.[23] Even in matters pertaining to local enlistments T'ang had wielded less authority than Lin Wei-yüan, a prominent and wealthy island-gentry figure commissioned to direct Taiwan's *t'uan* or militia forces upon Governor Shao's recommendation.[24]

In October, T'ang Ching-sung was appointed acting governor on the basis of the military reputation he had acquired in Annam some ten years previously at the time of the Sino-French War.[25] He immediately assumed full responsibility for defense preparations in Taiwan, as the throne had ordered him to do upon his appointment. However, in the course of his abrupt and inept handling of military affairs he apparently incurred the animosity of Admiral Yang, the influential gentry figure, Lin Wei-yüan, and most certainly that of Liu Yung-fu, whom he relegated to the extreme southern tip of the island.[26] Consequently, many mainland units stationed in Taiwan, including battalions of Huai, Hsiang, and Black Flag forces, became estranged from T'ang's effective control. T'ang worked out what he thought to be a partial remedy for this unsatisfactory situation by having raw Kwangtung levies shipped over from the mainland. He stationed these ill-trained units at strategic spots in northern areas of the island, but with disastrous results. The antics of the Kwangtung troops and their bandit-like leaders annoyed the inhabitants, lowered the morale of other military units in their vicinities, and largely accounted for the poor showing of the defense forces in northern Taiwan during the initial phase of the war.[27]

Although T'ang Ching-sung did not live up to his alleged military reputation while governor, his efforts to provide for Taiwan's defenses nonetheless netted some important accomplishments. At the outset of the Sino-Japanese War in 1894, only some twenty battalions (*ying*) totaling a few thousand troops were stationed on the island. Altogether, T'ang amassed a much larger standing force of 50,000 to 80,000 troops organized into well over two hundred battalions. He spread about three-fifths of these troops over northern Taiwan, correctly estimating that the Japanese would first concentrate their attack in that portion of the island as the French had done ten years previously.[28] He also was able to keep the arsenal and powder mill in the Taipei vicinity working at full capacity until shortly before the Japanese occupied that area. Again, T'ang managed to secure funds and provisions for Taiwan's defenses, ultimately through the assistance of his powerful supporter, Chang Chih-tung, then serving as acting governor-general in Nanking.[29]

The aid and advice rendered by Chang Chih-tung had an important bearing on T'ang's outlook and behavior as Taiwan's foremost resistance leader. Both T'ang and Chang actively negotiated through irregular channels in an effort to gain the support of England, France, and other European nations.[30] Their attempts to restore Taiwan to China by securing western aid or intervention encouraged T'ang to stay on at the head of the Taiwan government during the latter part of May. Moreover, his scheme to negotiate directly with western powers under the guise of an autonomous state led him to assume the title of president and inaugurate an island republic in Taipei on May 25, just four days before Japanese troops commenced to land on Taiwan.[31]

The story of T'ang's part in the creation of the Taiwan Republic has been dealt with in a separate study.[32] Here it is sufficient to relate that the republic proved to be merely a façade by which T'ang and his close associates dominated both civil and military affairs in northern Taiwan. Not a single western nation extended formal recognition to the new republic or advanced aid to the beleaguered island defenders. Meanwhile, the republic received little popular support even in the Taipei area. As the head of state, T'ang further alienated local gentry leaders and authorities who had favored self-rule for Taiwan.[33] Not only did many of the remaining Ch'ing officials now leave the island, but key defense authorities, such as Lin Wei-yüan, also soon departed from Taiwan.[34] The republic collapsed after only twelve days, when T'ang and his associates fled from Taipei. By then, conditions there had become so chaotic that any further resistance efforts in northern Taiwan appeared futile. Even though prior to his hasty departure T'ang had called upon Liu Yung-fu, Ch'iu Feng-chia, and other resistance leaders to send troops to Taipei, no such relief forces ever reached the capital.[35]

At the time of the downfall of the short-lived republic in Taipei, Ch'iu Feng-chia was undoubtedly the most influential resistance leader in the mid-island districts. Ch'iu proved responsible for much of the defensive build-up in that portion of Taiwan, much as T'ang Ching-sung had in the north. Ch'iu, however, held no administrative posts in government. He derived his influence through temporary military commissions and the active leadership roles he assumed among two important groups in Taiwanese society, the gentry and his fellow Hakkas.

Ch'iu was born and was reared in predominantly Hakka areas, formerly of the Chang-hua district, which had been included in the new Miao-li and Taiwan (Taichung) districts established in 1887.[36] One of the few island gentry ever to have attained the civil *chin-shih* degree, Ch'iu already had won local acclaim as a talented poet, scholar, and protégé of T'ang Ching-sung. In November, 1894, T'ang Ching-sung called upon Ch'iu to assist in the recruitment of local "volunteer braves" (*i-yung*) to bolster Taiwan's defenses. Ch'iu was duly commissioned and proceeded to raise battalions of volunteers.[37] These battalions were patterned after the *t'uan-lien* units then being mobilized by Lin Wei-yüan and other influential gentry members throughout the island. The battalions Ch'iu was instrumental in forming, however, consisted of Hakka troops. Apparently in order to differentiate between these Hakka battalions and the more common Hoklo *t'uan-lien* units, the term "*i-chün*" or "volunteer army" was devised for Ch'iu's forces.[38] There is evidence that Ch'iu sought to mobilize and assume command over an island-wide *i-chün* force. Nevertheless, by March his efforts had become confined mainly to the mid-island districts where he personally led such local Hakka units in defense preparations.[39]

At the head of his Hakka forces, Ch'iu Feng-chia developed into a powerful figure in his native areas of mid-

Taiwan. Late in April, Ch'iu reported that his estate in the Miao-li district was sheltering numerous local officials together with their secretaries and household members.[40] By May rumors even suggested that he was being hailed as "king" in the Chang-hua area.[41] Whether true or not, such rumors indicate that as conditions in Taiwan grew more unstable, Ch'iu emerged as a contender for power and authority on the island. His urgent pleas for self-rule and assertions that the inhabitants had been "abandoned" by the Ch'ing court indicate that Ch'iu was very much aware of the need for strong leadership in Taiwan.

Ch'iu's eminence as a resistance leader was enhanced by his contacts with local gentry members throughout the island. As soon as official news of the cession terms of the peace treaty belatedly reached Taiwan in the latter part of April, Ch'iu took the initiative in organizing gentry op-

position to the surrender of the island to Japan. Ch'iu addressed a strongly worded petition and other urgent pleas to the Ch'ing court, and launched a resistance movement in Taiwan which gained adherents in many areas.[42] His messages, included in Governor T'ang's memorials to the throne, were officially ignored in Peking, however, while his efforts to create an effective *i-chün* force failed to receive wholehearted support in Taipei. Chagrined at the court's ultimate decision to abide by the terms of the peace treaty and T'ang's evident shortcomings in respect to military affairs, Ch'iu eventually became a rival to the governor as a popular resistance leader.[43] When T'ang succeeded in elevating himself to the presidency of the Taiwan Republic late in May, Ch'iu evidently was reconciled by assurances that France would recognize the republic and intervene on its behalf. Although Ch'iu cooperated in helping to establish the republic, T'ang failed to grant him any title or office under the new government, as has oftentimes been reported.[44]

After the collapse of the republic and the loss of northern Taiwan, Ch'iu evidently gave up hope of resisting the Japanese advances in other portions of the island. Within a short time he left Taiwan for good. Nevertheless, his defiant spirit remained alive in the mid-island areas as indicated by the actions of some of his former officers in the *i-chün* forces. These young Hakka leaders offered resistance to the Japanese in areas extending from Hsin-chu south to the Chang-hua and Yün-lin districts.[45]

The Japanese occupation of northern Taiwan also failed to curb the spirit of resistance in the southern portion of the island. In fact, the loss of Taipei and T'ang Ching-sung's departure led to vigorous defensive measures in the Tainan area on the part of the bold and resourceful Black Flag leader, Liu Yung-fu.

At the outset of the war, Liu and his forces were still confined to the southern tip of Taiwan. There, Liu was held accountable for areas difficult to defend, yet forced to share his authority with the Taiwan brigade-general who held an equivalent title and the same rank. Although T'ang, on becoming president, had appointed Liu commander-in-chief of the republic, this promotion was of little consequence in southern Taiwan.[46] Liu and his forces remained isolated and relatively neglected until early in June when T'ang sent orders to march north and help relieve Taipei. T'ang's instructions were unrealistic in view of the distances involved and the precarious situation in the south. Liu wisely ignored them and proceeded to act on his own initiative. Instead of leading his forces far to the north, he shifted them to the strategic coastal areas extending from An-p'ing south to Takao (Kaohsiung). In so doing, he succeeded in filling what might be termed a power vacuum in the densely settled districts of southwestern Taiwan where the defenses were poorly organized and no other popular resistance leader had emerged. There, Liu and his forces were welcomed by the anxious inhabitants who wanted protection as well as order and stability in their communities.[47]

Liu soon was able to impose his authority over the southern districts of the island. In June he filled the vacated post of the Taiwan brigade-general located in the Tainan prefectural center. Accordingly, he moved his headquarters from the district seat of Feng-shan to Tainan-fu. Shortly thereafter, the Taiwan intendant, the highest ranking official in southern Taiwan, departed for the mainland, and the authority of that office devolved on Liu as well.[48] Already, in the absence of the Tainan prefect, Liu had begun to exercise stringent rule in those areas directly under his control. During the remainder of his four-month stay in Tainan he continued to adhere to severe measures so as to maintain order and provide for his troops. Liu also featured vestiges of the Taiwan Republic in Tainan to symbolize the resistance and elicit popular support. He convened a makeshift "parliament" (*i-yüan*) and eventually issued postage stamps and paper currency bearing the name of the republic.[49]

The severe measures and discipline Liu imposed in the Tainan area tarnished his image as a popular hero among the local inhabitants and troops under his command. Even so, he proved a key figure in the defense of southern Taiwan. So celebrated had Liu and his Black Flag forces become as dauntless warriors that the Japanese hesitated to attack Tainan without more troops at their disposal.[50] There is no question that his presence on the island helped to prolong the war, even though Liu, like T'ang Ching-sung, did not live up to the military reputation he had gained against the French in Annam. Eventually, on October 18, when the Japanese were about to launch a concerted attack on Tainan city, Liu also secretly fled back to the mainland.[51]

THE PREFECTURAL CENTERS AND REGIONAL RESISTANCE EFFORTS

The activities of these outstanding resistance leaders suggest that defense preparations varied in the three main portions of Taiwan. Further differences in the resistance efforts undertaken in each part of the island became apparent as the war progressed. Such dissimilarities were bound to prevail, for as the conflict shifted from the northern sector to mid-island and finally to the southern portions of Taiwan, other defense forces headed by different leaders entered the fray. Moreover, the three phases of the war occurred in regions corresponding roughly to the settled areas administered under each of Taiwan's three prefectures. The prefectural centers, normally serving as the key administrative centers of the island, then functioned as virtual wartime capitals within these respective regions. Each center in succession bore the brunt of the war and drew upon the available resources and manpower in that particular region, while carrying on armed resistance against the Japanese.

Although the resistance efforts differed in each region, there were marked similarities as well. By 1895, the island's administrative system on the prefectural level had acquired a rather uniform institutional pattern. Therefore, the authorities who bore wartime responsibilities at the three prefectural centers worked through equivalent governmental structures, and tended to resort to similar offices and systems of control existing within each prefecture. It is noteworthy that these three administrative centers were nearly on a par as far as their respective regional influence was concerned, despite evident variations in the type of civil and military offices situated at each seat of government. Thus, Taipei functioned as both the new provincial capital and the seat of the northern prefecture.[52] In practice, however, the governor and other provincial officials stationed in Taipei had never exercised real control over the entire island. By the spring of 1895, the authority of T'ang Ching-sung hardly transcended the bounds of the Taipei prefecture. Subsequently, during the first phase of the war Taipei functioned primarily as the wartime headquarters of Taiwan's northern region. Elsewhere, the much older town of Chang-hua served as the dominant administrative center for the recently established mid-island prefecture, while Tainan-fu, the original capital of the island, retained its predominance in southern Taiwan through the office of the Tainan prefect, together with the traditionally powerful Taiwan intendant and brigade-general posts still located there.

Under this arrangement, the resistance leader at the head of each center managed to exert a decisive influence over the major war efforts in his region. T'ang Ching-sung, who proved ineffective in a military role, was able for a time to retain a semblance of authority over the defenses in the north by controlling the allocation of funds and supplies from Taipei. In contrast, Liu Yung-fu was continually plagued by a lack of funds and provisions in Tainan, yet maintained considerable control over the troops in his region until near the end of the war by means of disciplinary actions and close supervision of the coastal defenses. In Chang-hua the prefect, Li Ching-sung, who assumed office in the early part of June, emerged as the chief resistance leader in the mid-island region after several powerful figures there, including Ch'iu Feng-chia, had quit Taiwan. As Japanese forces commenced to move southward from Taipei late in June, Li strove to rally the inhabitants and troops in his prefecture. He assumed the role of a popular leader, sought local gentry support, and endeavored to rival rather than cooperate with Liu Yung-fu in the south. In order to cope with the Japanese southward advance, as well as to outdo Liu as a military authority, Li also organized a separate resistance force, the Hsin Ch'u Army, comprised of many of the defense units remaining in his prefecture.[53]

Meanwhile, the authorities serving under these leaders at each of the three centers assumed the responsibility of supplying provisions for the resistance forces in their particular region. Taipei contained the provincial treasury, as well as the arsenal and powder mill. Hence, the units stationed in northern Taiwan tended to be relatively better armed and provisioned. In Chang-hua and Tainan the local gentry who managed the finances and supplies for the war effort had a more difficult task. Records indicate that they relied heavily on salt, likin, and customs duties, but also had to resort to more extraordinary means to gain revenue and provisions. The Chang-hua managers, for instance, sometimes confiscated the properties of wealthy inhabitants who had fled the scene.[54] In Tainan, both gentry and merchant representatives supported the issuance of postage stamps and paper currency, partly as a means to offset the methods of intimidation employed by Liu and his aides to collect funds and supplies.[55]

As the leaders and prefectural authorities undertook to carry on resistance efforts in their respective regions, they established separate defense offices in each center. Li Ching-sung and Liu Yung-fu set up emergency defense bureaus (*ch'ou-fang chü*) near their headquarters in Chang-hua and Tainan. Both modeled their bureaus after the Taipei office, bearing the same name, that had existed during T'ang Ching-sung's tenure as governor.[56] Each bureau functioned as a vital procurement and supply center, and operated under local gentry management.

Such emergency defense bureaus also served as meeting places where the leaders and their aides consulted with prominent gentry and wealthy merchants of the area.

A number of important matters relating to the resistance effort were resolved at such gatherings. It is significant that the secretive sessions which led to the formation of the Taiwan Republic in late May were held at the Taipei *ch'ou-fang chü*.[57] Again, Prefect Li Ching-sung met with the gentry managers of the Chang-hua bureau and discussed ways and means of raising funds and provisioning troops in that region.[58] In contrast, the Tainan emergency defense bureau may have played a somewhat less significant role as a place of contact between Liu Yung-fu and the southern gentry and merchants. On the whole, Liu and his aides seem to have maintained closer relations with the Tainan parliament. Nevertheless, they undoubtedly consulted with the bureau members as well. At least the prominent gentry figure heading that office could hardly have been ignored, so active was he in local defense matters.[59]

Other bureaus, similarly managed by island gentry and headquartered in each of Taiwan's three prefectural centers, also helped support local and regional resistance efforts both before and during the war. Two such types were the *pao-chia* and *t'uan-lien* bureaus. Unlike the emergency defense offices, these bureaus had functioned intermittently on the island over the previous decades whenever conditions there called for the extensive use of systems of local control and protection.[60]

In 1894, *t'uan-lien* bureaus were reactivated after Lin Wei-yüan was commissioned to direct the island's *t'uan* defenses (*t'uan-fang*). At that time the term "defense" referred to preparation for a possible Japanese attack. Accordingly, some effort was made to organize *yü-t'uan* units composed of coastal fishermen and their craft, along with regular *t'uan-lien* militia forces.[61] However, when conditions grew chaotic in Taiwan, local defense authorities tended to concentrate primarily on the task of affording protection from internal strife. *T'uan-lien* bureaus and branches proliferated about the island as wealthy gentry set about organizing and financing local battalions of "drilled braves" (*lien-yung*) to safeguard their communities, or in some cases merely their own properties. Despite the fact that Lin was supposed to direct the *t'uan* defenses, no effective overall chain of command was devised to weld the *t'uan-lien* bureaus and battalions throughout Taiwan into an integrated local defense system.[62]

In the long run, the *t'uan-lien* bureaus in the mid-island and southern portions of Taiwan did contribute something to the resistance efforts in their regions. In Chang-hua the operations of the *t'uan-lien* and *pao-chia* bureaus were merged; and local gentry, more responsive to the dictates of the prefectural bureau managers, began to be assigned to battalions of trained militia in their areas. As a result, the revamped bureau in Chang-hua soon had better organized and more mobile units at its disposal to offer protection against banditry throughout the mid-island districts. Although such forces were not used against the Japanese, they enabled the processes of government and the vital wartime activities to proceed in a more orderly manner.[63] Elsewhere, the Tainan *t'uan-lien* bureau also was able to mold the battalions of local troops in and around that city into an effective protective force. These units proved able to quell insurgent elements in the surrounding countryside as well as maintain order in Tainan-fu itself.[64]

In the spring of 1895, *pao-chia* offices were established or reactivated in Taiwan in an even more haphazard manner than were the *t'uan-lien* bureaus. Most of these offices commenced to function when local authorities grew alarmed over the increase of banditry and disorder. Then such bureaus and local systems mushroomed in district seats and market towns about the island. Even villages cooperated to form "united village offices" (*lien-chuang chü*) comparable to *pao-chia* bureaus.[65] Early in April efforts were made by the mid-island prefect to establish a main *pao-chia* headquarters in Chang-hua. This office was named the "united *chia* bureau" (*lien-chia chü*) and at first attempted to set up a system of mutual protection in the town of Chang-hua and its environs, bolstered by a small standing force of trained militia. Several months later when this office was merged with the prefectural *t'uan-lien* bureau, its protective functions were improved and extended over a much wider area.[66]

In September several aides of Liu Yung-fu proposed a further use for a similar type of *pao-chia* network. They advocated that the local "braves" (*yung*) throughout the island be enrolled in a united village *pao-chia* system with headquarters in Tainan. According to their reasoning, a large resistance force stretching from Tainan all the way north to Taipei would thus be formed to combat the Japanese in the south as well as elsewhere in the occupied areas of Taiwan. Liu Yung-fu endorsed this plan but was never able to put it into effect.[67]

The fact that Liu and his aides envisioned directing such an extensive network of rural forces from their headquarters in Tainan indicates that they were concerned with widespread resistance efforts of an inter-regional scope, which the chief resistance leaders did indeed carry on. T'ang Ching-sung, for example, made decisions affecting the defenses of the entire island even though his actual authority was limited mainly to the northern portion. Later on, after the loss of Taipei, both Li Ching-sung and Liu Yung-fu extended their operations farther to the north beyond their respective regions in hope of curbing the Japanese advance southward and even rolling back the occupation forces.[68] In their roles as inter-regional, if not actual island-wide resistance leaders, both Li and Liu also saw fit to request aid from Chinese officials on the mainland. Following the example of T'ang Ching-sung, they addressed most of their pleas to Chang Chih-tung but received only negative replies in return.[69]

At times, the activities of local gentry in one or another of the three key centers also extended beyond the bounds of their particular regions. Lin Wei-yüan, for example, was responsible for the *t'uan* defenses throughout the entire island as well as those in his native Taipei area. During the war, too, gentry managers of the various wartime bureaus sometimes engaged in inter-regional efforts. In mid-July, for example, the anxious managers of the Chang-hua emergency defense bureau petitioned Liu Yung-fu to send troops north to their area. A month later managers of that center's united *chia* bureau requested relief rations from the Tainan *pao-chia* bureau. In both cases the pleas of these Chang-hua gentry were heeded, and troops as well as supplies were duly sent north from Tainan.[70]

While the resistance efforts emanating from each prefectural center assumed inter-regional dimensions, other defense activities of an intra-regional nature also took shape among districts within the prefectures. Some district seats of government, in fact, developed into minor wartime centers. There, the authorities, headed as a rule by an acting magistrate, directed the defensive operations staged in or beyond their districts as best they could. The importance of the district seats during the war depended not only on their relative strategic value, but on their background and location as administrative seats as well. Hence, the seat of the Yün-lin district, relocated at Tou-liu only two years previously, could muster only a small force in defense of the immediate vicinity. In contrast, the much older district seat of Chia-i, located directly to the south, proved a more active center of local defense preparations.[71] It is also noteworthy that the two long-established district seats of Chia-i and Hsin-chu, both located midway between prefectural centers in what might be termed regional border areas, fostered relatively independent resistance efforts.[72]

Nevertheless, the prefectural centers, rather than the district seats, played largely major roles in the resistance. The relative importance of the prefectural centers is suggested by the actions of Liu Yung-fu, who in his efforts to assume control over the southern Taiwan defenses, shifted his headquarters from the remote district seat of Heng-ch'un to the more strategic seat at Feng-shan, then soon afterwards to the key center of Tainan-fu where the institutions of regional control existed.

THE WAR AND THE RESISTANCE FORCES

A brief description of the war and the resistance forces active in each of its three phases reveals more clearly the vital wartime roles of Taiwan's prefectural centers. In all, the leadership and material support forthcoming from these centers enabled a sustained war to be waged in the more densely settled districts of the island. Without the presence of the resistance leaders, their aides, and the gentry managers at these key administrative centers it is doubtful whether more than sporadic actions by local armed bodies would have been forthcoming in most lowland areas of Taiwan during the Japanese take-over.

Nevertheless, these centers were able to exercise only limited control over the war efforts in their particular regions. To begin with, the authorities in the prefectural centers operated under adverse conditions which severely hampered their activities. Poor transportation facilities, a lack of funds and provisions, the prevailing banditry and turmoil, and varying responses to the war and occupation on the part of the local inhabitants proved to be among the chief impediments. Again, not all the numerous forces which offered opposition to the Japanese at one time or another during the war were supported or even recognized by the authorities of each center. Many defense units were entirely dependent on the backing of particular districts, towns, villages, or even powerful families and individuals.

The first phase of the war fought in northern Taiwan illustrates the vital, though restricted, role of the authorities in that region's key administrative center. T'ang Ching-sung had assumed personal charge of the defense preparations there, and Taipei remained the source of funds and supplies for the military. Neither T'ang nor his aides, however, exercised much overall authority over the leaders of the resistance forces scattered about the north. Following the practice of his predecessor, Governor Shao, T'ang simply commissioned various military figures with several battalions at their disposal as "commanders" (*t'ung-ling.*)[73] All such commanders were of equal rank and acted as virtually autonomous military authorities in their particular areas. During the short struggle in northern Taiwan this practice proved disastrous, particularly in respect to the Kwangtung units involved. The Taipei authorities were unable to direct a coordinated defensive effort, while the commanders and their unruly troops acted according to their own inclinations.[74]

The war commenced on May 29, when units of Japan's Imperial Guard division landed at the secluded area of Ao-ti, some twenty miles southeast of Keelung. This landing force encountered light resistance, and by June 3 was able to occupy the port town of Keelung. The defense forces assigned to guard Keelung and the strategic mountainous terrain to the west consisted mainly of ill-trained Kwangtung units that had only recently arrived in Taiwan. Their meagre resistance proved futile, and four days later a small Japanese force marched inland and occupied Taipei. During this time, T'ang's trusted aides were unable to restore order among the defense units in the Keelung and Taipei areas, while T'ang himself could not be persuaded to assume personal command over his ineffective troops.[75] By the time the harbor town of Tan-shui fell to the Japanese on June 9, resistance in the north had collapsed. The chaos that resulted in Taipei and its environs before the occupation forces arrived suggests that no extended system of local control had been organized in northern Taiwan under T'ang's leadership.[76]

The loss of northern Taiwan constituted a severe setback to the resistance forces in other parts of the island. The best-equipped defense units in Taiwan, including most of the Chinese mainland troops, surrendered with the fall of Taipei and Tan-shui. The bulk of the public funds also were lost to the war effort when the provincial treasury in Taipei was looted by a frenzied mob. In addition, the island's only arsenal and only powder mill were destroyed by vandals.[77] Consequently, the resistance leaders and defense units to the south were left to their own devices in amassing troops, funds, and supplies.

Furthermore, the loss of the north, and especially the fall of Taipei, thoroughly discouraged a number of key figures who had been active in the resistance efforts up to that time. Ch'iu Feng-chia and another powerful mid-island gentry figure, Lin Ch'ao-tung, both quit the island, as did the Fukien authority, Yang Ju-i, who had been in charge of the troops and defenses in the Chang-hua and Taiwan (Taichung) districts.[78] The departure of these three figures represented a further setback for the resistance effort, since they commanded the bulk of the standing defense forces in the districts directly south of the occupied Taipei area.

Meanwhile, the Japanese were jubilant over their easy take-over of northern Taiwan. Confident that organized resistance would soon subside throughout the island once the capital had been seized, Governor-General Kabayama Sukenori officially inaugurated his new government in Taipei (Taihoku) amid festivities on June 17.[79] Immediate preparations were then made to occupy the districts to the south. On June 19, Imperial Guard units started from the capital and within three days had seized their first main objective, the district seat of Hsin-chu.[80] Elsewhere, on the east coast an auxiliary force composed of Ōsaka Fourth Division reserves staged landings in the I-lan district on June 21, and in only two days' time had peacefully entered the main towns of Lo-tung and I-lan in that area.[81]

Despite the ease with which their forces continued to sweep over areas of the island, the Japanese military authorities grew concerned before long that the occupation of Taiwan might prove lengthier and more costly than anticipated. There had been a delay in the arrival of equipment that would have permitted a second major landing in the Tainan vicinity early in June. The southwest monsoon season was already at hand, a factor which made operations in the Taiwan Strait extremely hazardous during the summer months. Hence, the Imperial Guards were ordered to proceed overland through the western coastal areas towards their ultimate objective, Tainan city.[82] As Imperial Guard forces set out from the Taipei vicinity, however, a more spirited type of resistance was encountered. Along the route to the south their rear supply columns came under the attack of local guerrilla bands. Then, when the district seat of Hsin-chu was taken, the occupation force that had entered the town was bottled up by an array of newly formed defense units. Subsequently, the Japanese advance southward was stalled for over a month and a half in the Hsin-chu district.

The defense forces that entered the war as the Japanese neared Hsin-chu are of interest, for they differed markedly from the units that had offered only token resistance to the north. Basically, these forces consisted of three main types. First, there were *i-yung* battalions comprised of local recruits from the mid-island districts. Some were seasoned Hoklo battalions which had served under Lin Ch'ao-tung and remained intact after Lin's departure. Others were newly formed units with no previous military experience. Still other battalions consisted of Hakka volunteers and by and large were remnants of Chiu Feng-chia's *i-chün* force. Such Hakka units at times proved the most effective in carrying on guerrilla warfare against the Japanese.[83]

All of these various Hoklo and Hakka volunteer battalions apparently were organized in about the same manner as Taiwan's *t'uan-lien* units. They can be distinguished from the latter type of unit by their battalion names and the fact that their troops were designated as "volunteer braves" (*i-yung*) in contrast to the "drilled braves" (*lien-yung*) maintained by wealthy gentry and the *t'uan-lien* bureaus. This distinction between volunteer and drilled braves oftentimes became blurred during the war, but ordinarily the *i-yung* units functioned as local standing defense forces while the *lien-yung* troops served as reserves and only protected their own localities from banditry and disorder. In the Hsin-chu district and the mid-island prefecture the more mobile *i-yung* units seem to have received provisions from Chang-hua and authorities in nearby district seats. In July and August, while the Hsin Ch'u Army was active, a number of these volunteer

Hoklo and Hakka battalions cooperated with that body.[84]

The Hsin Ch'u Army constituted the second type of resistance force that operated against the Japanese in the Hsin-chu area. This army, organized in June by Li Ching-sung with the active support of local gentry and wealthy inhabitants of the four mid-island districts, was formed around the Ch'u and Hsiang military commanders and units remaining in mid-Taiwan. Altogether, the Hsin Ch'u Army comprised some fourteen battalions, and probably numbered around 7,000 troops.[85] With this army, Li Ching-sung attempted to drive the Japanese from Hsin-chu by ordering a series of counterattacks against that town between July 9 and 24. These desperate attacks proved futile and succeeded only in weakening the Hsin Ch'u Army and depleting the meager funds and supplies available in the mid-island prefecture, as the Chang-hua gentry managers had forewarned.[86]

The makeup of the resistance forces in the Hsin-chu district and areas to the south became more complex as local *i-min* or partisan bands began to carry on guerrilla operations against the Japanese. Such partisan bands constituted the third main type of resistance unit that arose during the second phase of the war, yet they did not fit well into the prefectural or district patterns of defense. Not only did these bands often fail to heed the commands of the local authorities, but they tended to compete for the slender rations available to the resistance forces in each area as well. The *i-min* band that ultimately proved most outstanding in the mid-island region happened to be a Hakka force and raised further problems. In Hsin-chu the inhabitants of the district seat did not trust armed Hakkas from Miao-li. Eventually, the leader of this formidable band, Wu T'ang-hsing, even quarreled with the magistrate of his home district over pay for his men. In spite of the troubles that beset Wu and his followers, this partisan band offered spirited resistance against the Japanese until late August when Wu was killed in the defense of Chang-hau.[87]

During his career as an *i-min* leader Wu T'ang-hsing claimed to be the commander of an island-wide partisan force.[88] Actually, no such extensive force was ever organized, nor did other partisan bands that emerged later acknowledge Wu as their leader. As the war continued, these bands included more lawless elements within their ranks until finally the desperate Tainan authorities began to recruit self-styled *i-min* bands headed by known bandit chiefs.[89] Such partisan bands invariably proved of little benefit to the war effort although some made brief, spirited stands in their own localities.

It was a conglomeration of partisan bands, Hsin Ch'u units, and local volunteer battalions that held up the Imperial Guard forces in the Hsin-chu district for over a month and a half. At the district seat some 2,000 Japanese troops defended the town against the sporadic attacks of a resistance force probably over five times that size. To the north, other Japanese units fought local guerrilla bands in an effort to pacify the area and maintain communications between Taipei and the besieged town of Hsin-chu. However, by the end of July, as sizable Japanese reinforcements and supplies reached Hsin-chu, the tide of battle turned heavily in favor of the Imperial Guards. Areas in the northern parts of the district were secured, and the main Imperial Guard force began to make a wide sweep southward during the first week in August.[90]

Although the fighting in the Hsin-chu district turned out to be the severest of the war, the Imperial Guards emerged much stronger than before. In particular, they gained a heavy preponderance in weapons and fire power, advantages the Japanese were to enjoy for the remainder of the war. After the resistance efforts in Hsin-chu had seriously depleted the local resources available for the defense of the mid-island perfecture, the Japanese were able to take over most of the mid-Taiwan region during the month of August. On the fourteenth of August the district seat of Miao-li was captured without resistance.[91] To the south, the main defense units of the region combined forces in order to make a last-ditch stand at the prefectural center of Chang-hua. Strong positions were taken on Pa-kua Mountain guarding the northern approaches to that town. Nevertheless, in a single battle, on August 28, the Japanese, by means of a well-executed stratagem, managed to drive the defenders from the mountain and seize Chang-hua along with the nearby port town of Lu-kang.[92]

The celebrated battle of Pa-kua Mountain marked the climax of the second phase of the war. The main defense force of mid-Taiwan was vanquished, and the key administrative center of Chang-hua was turned into a military headquarters for the Imperial Guards. In the mid-island coastal region only Yün-lin, the southern-most district, remained unoccupied. There, as well as in the Chia-i district farther to the south, another conglomeration of defense units gathered to continue the resistance.[93]

Not until October 3, did the main forces of the Imperial Guards at Chang-hua commence to push south once again.[94] By then, the Japanese were about to enter upon the third phase of the war and converge on Tainan by sea as well as by land. The monsoon period has passed, and Japan's Second Division was assembling at the Pescadores in preparation for landings to be staged at points to the north and south of the Tainan and An-p'ing area. The advance of the Imperial Guards overland was planned in conjunction with these landings.[95]

Against such superior forces, the beleaguered defenders in the southern portion of Taiwan were relatively helpless. The Imperial Guards met with occasional stubborn resistance on the part of *i-yung* and *i-min* forces, supported by Black Flag detachments, as they drove southward toward the Yün-lin and Chia-i districts early in October. Nonetheless, their advance was rapid. The district seat of Yün-lin (Tou-liu) fell on October 7, and the important center of Chia-i two days later. After a brief rest, the Imperial Guards pushed to a place within ten miles of Tainan city on the twentieth.[96]

By that time units of the Second Division already had staged their landings along the southwest coast and made rapid advances against areas under Liu Yung-fu's command. On October 10, that division's Fourth Mixed Brigade landed about twenty-eight miles north of Tainan-fu near Pu-tai, then proceeded to fan southward. By the sixteenth this force had pressed within striking distance of the Tainan and An-p'ing area from the north.[97] Meanwhile, on October 11, the rest of the Second Division landed unopposed near Fang-liao some twenty-five miles south of Takao. This force proceeded north, occupying the town of Tung-kang on the twelfth and the district seat of Feng-shan on the fifteenth.[98] Altogether, about 12,000 Japanese troops engaged in these two landings, while Liu Yung-fu's forces, one totaling around 30,000, had begun to dwindle at a rapid pace.

Initially, the Japanese appeared cautious in their southern campaign. Both landings were purposely made at spots beyond the areas where Liu's Black Flag units were known to be stationed. Actually, as it turned out, the Japanese had overestimated the Black Flags as a military force. The Black Flag battalions probably numbered less than 4,000 troops, and many of these were rather old men brought over from Kwangtung, or else new enlistments recruited in Taiwan and the mainland.[99] As the Japanese converged on the well-fortified coastal areas manned by

Black Flag units, the lack of fighting zeal among Liu's men became evident. On October 15, Japanese naval units easily seized Takao and its fortifications, where a sizable Black Flag force was stationed. These units fled to Tainan city, as happened in other instances when the occupation forces neared Black Flag installations.[100] In effect, the sporadic opposition encountered by the various Japanese forces as they converged on the Tainan area came mainly from local volunteer units and partisan bands, as well as possibly from a few Hsiang and Huai troops remaining in the region. Again, during the last days before Tainan fell, the local *t'uan-lien* battalions maintained order in that besieged city. After Liu Yung-fu and his entourage had escaped on the eighteenth, these battalions helped to hand the city over to the Japanese three days later without any major incident.[101]

Following the surrender of Tainan on October 21, Governor-General Kabayama declared that Taiwan had been pacified.[102] His proclamation was premature, however, for areas to the south of Takao as well as regions in the central highlands and along the eastern coastline of the island had not yet been occupied. Moreover, the Japanese were to encounter further armed resistance from Hakka bands in the southern Heng-ch'un district, then soon afterwards experience desperate partisan attacks near the end of 1895 and during the first part of 1896.[103] In fact, bandit-like partisan bands continued to plague the Japanese until 1902.[104] Nonetheless, Kabayama was correct in assuming that the main work of pacification had been completed with the surrender of Tainan. The takeover of Taiwan's last key center of resistance meant that prolonged defensive warfare, carried on mainly through the existing prefectural framework of the late Ch'ing period, was no longer feasible on the island.

The 1895 Taiwan War of Resistance

THE WAR IN HISTORICAL PERSPECTIVE

Viewed in retrospect, the Taiwan war of resistance marks an important juncture in the island's history. Just as Taiwan had acquired provincial status and was becoming a more integral part of imperial China, it was ceded to Japan as new territory for the Japanese empire. The cession turned out not to be a peaceful transfer of China's island province, as the Ch'ing and Meiji governments had desired. Instead, sustained warfare ensued in Taiwan before the island passed completely into Japanese hands and the local patterns of Chinese authority ceased to function there.

As indicated above, this 1895 war proved to be a self-contained conflict distinct from the Sino-Japanese War that had preceded it. Actually, the Ch'ing court, fearful of becoming embroiled in a Taiwan incident with Japan, had taken steps beforehand to assure that any such armed resistance to the impending take-over would remain a separate conflict isolated from China. On the whole the court succeeded in keeping the struggle in Taiwan detached from China, despite the continued presence of a few Chinese officials and a number of mainland military units on the island during the war. Few supplies and apparently no troop reinforcements reached Taiwan after the outbreak of hostilities there. Meanwhile, the Peking authorities officially ignored the war, refused to recognize the Taiwan Republic, and declined to answer all memorials and dispatches the resistance leaders sent from the island.[105]

Although the Taiwan war remained detached from China proper, it nevertheless falls within the purview of Chinese local history. The conflict, after all, took place in an area which retained the semblance of a province of imperial China, and involved resistance on the part of

Chinese who still professed to be loyal Ch'ing subjects. Moreover, the war was fought within a diverse social setting not markedly different from conditions in the mainland provinces of southeastern China. There, too, tension still prevailed between the local Hakka population and other Chinese indigenous to these regions, while the inhabitants of such mainland areas likewise remained set apart from one another due to dissimilarities in language and custom as well as the existence of natural barriers formed by mountainous terrain. Such conditions were especially evident in Fukien and Kwangtung, provinces from which the vast majority of Taiwan's inhabitants emanated.[106]

In Taiwan the disparate social conditions prevailing there hampered resistance efforts throughout the island during 1895. The lack of cohesion and harmony among the local inhabitants ruled out the possibility of a concerted defense based upon widespread popular support. Neither the chief resistance leaders nor the short-lived republic, that supposedly had symbolized island-wide unity, succeeded in securing extensive backing. By early June, after northern Taiwan had fallen, those inhabitants who did support the resistance effort seem to have been more interested in protecting their own home areas than in defending the island as a whole against the Japanese. Evidence shows that they were particularly concerned over the dire consequences which they imagined the Japanese occupation would bring to their own groups and localities.[107]

To be sure, prominent island leaders alleged that strong local indignation over the surrender of Taiwan to Japan had prompted their resistance efforts in 1895. Both T'ang Ching-sung and Liu Yung-fu alluded to the aroused inhabitants as if an intense spirit of patriotism and even nationalism (represented by the evident anti-Japanese sentiment) had pervaded the island's Chinese population. Meanwhile, Ch'iu Feng-chia constantly referred to the anger and defiance expressed by Taiwan's "gentry and people."[108] The popular resentment that these resistance leaders portrayed was perhaps indicative of the general mood current on the island after the cession terms of the peace treaty became known. However, it must be remembered that all three of these resistance leaders were attempting to impress the authorities on the mainland as well as incite the local populace to action by means of such stirring pronouncements. They failed to mention the diverse background and localized outlook of the inhabitants as factors which precluded the effective utilization of any such widespread indignation for concerted action against the Japanese, at least under the turbulent conditions that prevailed on the island at the time.

Neither did these resistance leaders refer in public to the lack of strong centralized authority on the island. Nevertheless, each realized that the existing controls on the provincial level of government were too weak to bring about a well-integrated, island-wide defensive effort. T'ang Ching-sung, while governor and president, seemed especially aware of the limits to his authority in southern Taiwan. His messages dated prior to the outbreak of hostilities, in fact, suggest that he eventually shunned responsibility for the defenses in the southern portion of the island.[109] Then during March and April even T'ang's influence in the mid-Taiwan districts declined appreciably. Thereafter, none of the other resistance leaders were able or willing to overcome the problem of decentralized authority on the island. As a consequence, the war of resistance came to be waged mainly on a prefectural rather than a provincial basis under circumstances which, ironically, enabled the struggle to continue much longer than would probably have been the case had Taiwan's defenses been more dependent on central authority stemming from Taipei.

While treating with the Taiwan war of resistance in the context of local Chinese history, one should also relate this conflict to the general scene of nineteenth-century China. Viewed from this perspective, the war proves to have been still another effort on the part of local Chinese defenders to ward off the forces of a formidable foreign nation during the late Ch'ing period. All such inglorious wars that China waged against the various world powers, beginning with the outbreak of the Opium War in 1839, amounted to provincial or at most regional conflicts rather than national wars involving the whole of China and her resources. This particular struggle against Japan fits well within this category of limited defensive actions.[110]

The Taiwan war exemplifies in many other ways the foreign wars in which China engaged during the nineteenth century. For one thing, this conflict, like the Sino-French and Sino-Japanese wars preceding it, reflects the influence of self-strengthening policies which had led to a more general use of western-type weapons and equipment in China over the latter decades of that century. In Taiwan reforms related to the island's defenses had begun in the 1870s when modern Armstrong and Krupp guns were first installed in coastal locations there.[111] Later, Liu Ming-ch'uan launched other major undertakings, including the construction of an arsenal, powder-mill, and railroad, which figured heavily in the defenses of northern Taiwan.[112] Hence, as a result of attempts to modernize China's military forces on both the island and mainland, many of the regular troops assigned to Taiwan in 1894–1895 were equipped with western firearms. On the other hand, as in previous wars, some defense forces active during the Taiwan conflict were mostly armed with old-fashioned weapons, such as Chinese pikes, spears, and gingals. Many local volunteer units tended to be so equipped.[113]

This contrast in the use of new and old-fashioned arms suggests the diverse types of defense units employed during the war of resistance. Along with other areas of China threatened by attack during the nineteenth century, Taiwan had gradually acquired more modern-type military forces to supplement the old-style ones still in use there. In the 1880s, for example, semi-modern Hsiang and Huai battalions permanently replaced Green Standard units as Taiwan's regular defense forces.[114] The latter remnants of earlier centuries of Ch'ing rule were not used during the war of resistance, while mainland battalions patterned after the former type of semi-modern army units saw limited action. Some of the local *i-yung* forces that fought the Japanese following the take-over of northern

Taiwan also were of a relatively recent vintage, at least as far as their battalion organization was concerned. Such volunteer forces could hardly be described as modern, though, no more than could the island's *t'uan-lien* battalions which gained official support in Taiwan during the latter half of the century. Finally, the protective bands of *i-min* and *pao-chia* defenders, formed during the second and third phases of the war, had long served as types of local emergency forces on the strife-ridden Taiwan scene.[115] These bands, in terms of their arms and makeup, might be labeled strictly old-fashioned. However, the *pao-chia* bureaus represented more recent advances in organizational and training procedure, as well as reflected the propensity of Chinese on both the island and the mainland to form *ad hoc* bureaus whenever emergencies arose during the late Ch'ing period.[116]

These diverse types of defense units which functioned during the Taiwan war represent the more typical military and protective forces that had come to operate in China by the time of the French and Japanese wars. Although neither modern nor very effective against well-trained foreign troops, as the history of the nineteenth century indicates, the newer forms of defense forces at least denote military change in China from the time of the Opium War. One may note that during the Taiwan war this order of change was reversed as far as the resistance forces were concerned. The bulk of the semimodern and better equipped defense units dropped out of the conflict during the first phase. After that, with the exception of portions of the Hsin Ch'u Army to the north and the Black Flag units manning the coastal batteries in the southwest, the resistance forces that confronted the Japanese consisted mainly of old-style local volunteer units.

These local units attempted to ward off the Japanese advance in much the same manner as similar Taiwan defense forces had done previously against sizable rebel bands. Considering the lack of centralized authority, apathy on the part of the majority of the inhabitants, and disparate social groupings among the local Chinese, the prolonged resistance carried on by such means was a remarkable feat. This protective action undoubtedly would have been adequate to quell most any of the extensive rebellions that had ravaged Taiwan in the past. Against the much superior forces of a nation like Japan such localized action, of course, was bound to fail. Nevertheless, organized resistance was waged against Japanese occupation forces for nearly five months, though no outside help was forthcoming, even from China, and the defenders had to depend on the dwindling resources available in Taiwan itself.

THE 1895
JAPANESE TAKE-OVER
of
TAIWAN
(Dates of Military Actions)

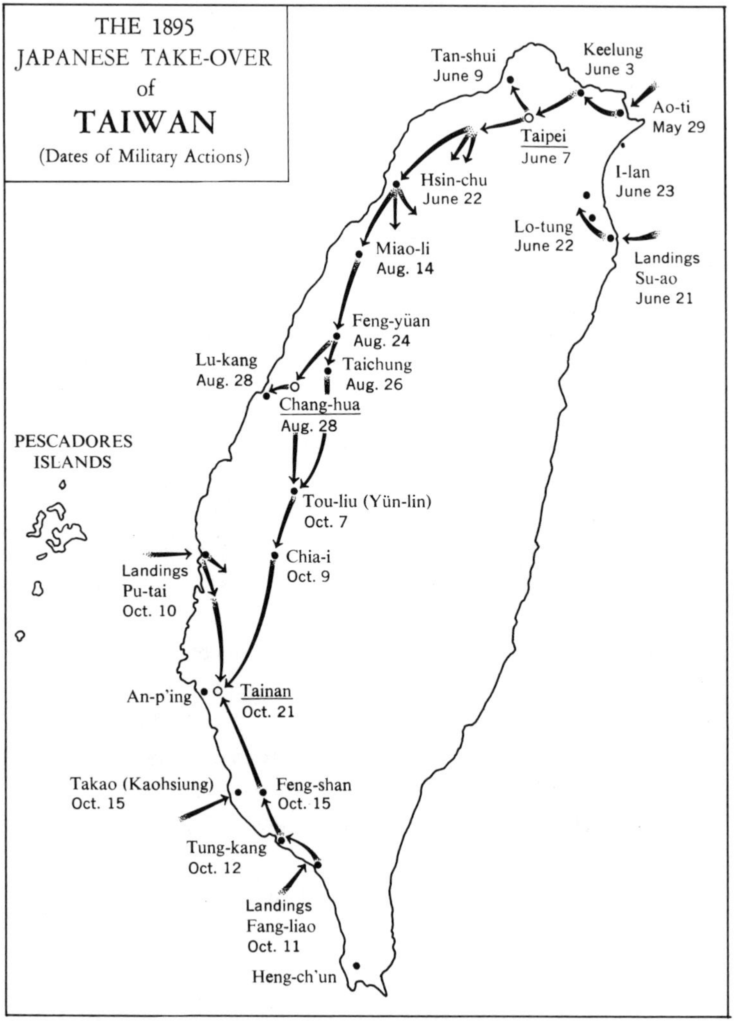

Notes

1. Several scholars in Taiwan also have distinguished between the Sino-Japanese War of 1894–1895 and the Taiwan war of 1895. Ch'en Han-kuang maintains that the former war involved two nations, while the latter was between two peoples, the Chinese and the Japanese. Ch'en Han-kuang, "I-wei chih chan yü Chung-kuo shih-t'an" (The war of 1895 and the field of Chinese poetry), *T'ai-pei wen-wu*, IX, 1 (March, 1960), 90. Liao Han-ch'en contends that the Sino-Japanese War took place according to Ch'ing imperial dictates before the peace treaty. The Taiwan war came after the peace treaty in defiance of such dictates. Liao Han-ch'en, "Chia-wu chih i tsai wen-t'an shang ti fanying" (Reflections of the 1894-1895 war in the field of literature), *T'ai-wan wen-hsien*, VII, 1-2 (June, 1956), 93.

2. The first such instructions were sent to Chang Chih-tung on May 15. Other decrees with more explicit instructions forbidding arms, rations, and troops to be sent to Taiwan were issued to Chang and other officials on May 28 and June 2. T'ai-wan yin-hang, ching-chi shih (Bank of Taiwan, Bureau of Economics), comp., *Ch'ing Te-tsung shih-lu hsüan-chi* (Selections from the *shih-lu* of the Ch'ing emperor, Te-tsung) (Taipei, 1964), II, 299 (KH21/4/21), and 302 (5/5 and 5/10). Hereafter cited as *SLHC*.

3. *SLHC*, II, 301 (KH21/4/26).

4. It was deemed unsafe for the commissioner, Li Ching-fang, the nephew and adopted son of Li Hung-chang, to set foot on Taiwan by that late date. Hence, he met with the Japanese representatives aboard ship. Hosea Ballou Morse, *Letter-books (1886-1907)* MS (Houghton Library, Harvard), III, letter 1306 (June 3, 1895); and James W. Davidson, *The Island of Formosa Past and Present* (Yokohama, 1903), pp. 292-95.

5. This term or ones similar to it appear in the Japanese records and literature of the period. For example, see Governor-General Kabayama's report of November 18, 1895, contained in Sugiyama Seiken, *Taiwan rekidai sōtoko no*

chiseki (Administrative record of Taiwan's successive governors-general) (Tokyo, 1922), p. 27.

6. I have attempted to show something of Taiwan's development during the latter part of the nineteenth century in connection with the rise of the local gentry in an unpublished dissertation. Harry Jerome Lamley, "The Taiwan Literati and Early Japanese Rule, 1895-1915: A Study of Their Reactions to the Japanese Occupation and Subsequent Responses to Colonial Rule and Modernization" (University of Washington, 1964), esp. pp. 81-132.

7. In 1862, the Hsin-chu gentry scholar, Lin Chan-mei, was allowed to form a *t'uan-lien* militia corps in his area. Previous to this the local authorities had disapproved of the use of such local forces in Taiwan. Thereafter, however, the island officials began to encourage the formation of these militia units for local protection. T'ai-wan sheng wen-hsien wei-yüan-hui (Taiwan provincial historical commission), comp., *T'ai-wan sheng t'ung-chih kao* (Draft gazetteer of Taiwan province), chüan 3, *Cheng-shih chih*; *Pao-an p'ien* (Records of political affairs; Section on peace preservation (Taipei, 1959), pp. 143-47. This draft gazetteer is hereafter cited as *T'ung-chih kao.*

8. *T'ung-chih kao, chüan* 3, *Cheng-shih chih; Fang-shu p'ien* (Records of political affairs; Section on defense) (Taipei, 1959), pp. 106-108, 162.

9. Liu Ming-ch'uan's defense of northern Taiwan and his reforms as governor are dealt with in Davidson, pp. 221-56. See also Samuel C. Chu, "Liu Ming-ch'uan and Modernization of Taiwan," *The Journal of Asian Studies,* XXIII, 1 (Nov., 1963), 39-53. The more traditional kinds of reform Liu endeavored to carry out are covered in Inō Yoshinari, *Taiwan-Jimbu to shite no Ryū Meiden* (Liu Ming-ch'uan as governor of Taiwan) (Taihoku, 1905), pp. 54-93.

10. The two and a half divisions included the Imperial Guards, the Second Division, and reserves from the Osaka Fourth Division. Davidson, pp. 353-54. The exact number of Japanese troops sent to Taiwan during the war varies in different accounts. Ch'en Han-kuang sets the figure at 70,049,

including the coolies. See his *T'ai-wan k'ang-Jih shih* (History of Taiwan's resistance to Japan) (Taipei, 1948), p. 52.

11. Estimates of the units and number of troops that made up the total defense force vary considerably. Ch'en's figures would total over 120,000. Ch'en, p. 2. However, T'ang Ching-sung claimed to have 150,000 troops under his command at the outset of the war. Davidson, p. 286. The Taiwanese historian, Lien Heng (Ya-t'ang), maintained that the island's total resistance force comprised over 300 battalions, with 360 men to each battalion. Lien Heng, *T'ai-wan t'ung-shih* (General history of Taiwan) (Taipei, 1955, reprint), p. 70.

12. The casualty figures cited by Davidson are usually followed by Japanese authors, while Chinese writers tend to set the total losses sustained by the Japanese at a higher rate. See Davidson, pp. 364-66; and, for example, the table appended to the Chinese translation of a book by Sigiura Wasaku reentitled, *Ch'ing-mo Jih-chün kung T'ai chi* (Record of the Japanese military attack on Taiwan at the end of the Ch'ing period) (n.p., n.d.), p. 115. Davidson claims that altogether both sides lost over 12,000 men as the result of wounds and disease. His figures indicate that the casualties caused by disease were extremely high. The Japanese lost 4,642 men in Taiwan because of sickness. In addition, 5,246 others were confined to hospitals in Taiwan, and 21,748 were sent to Japan for treatment.

13. The suffering of the civilian population in Taiwan is not well documented. Glimpses of the chaos and deplorable conditions of the time may be gained from the poetry written by local scholars during the period, as well as from the more reliable contemporary accounts of the conflict. See especially the two accounts: Hung Ch'i-sheng (I-chih), *Ying-hai hsieh-wang chi* (Record of those deserted in the great sea) (Taipei, 1959, reprint); and Wu Te-kung, *Jang T'ai chi* (Record of the surrender of Taiwan), reprinted in T'ai-wan yin-hang ching-chi shih, comp., *Ke T'ai san-chi* (Three records of the cession of Taiwan) (Taipei, 1959), pp. 31-73. For some of the epidemics that raged in Taiwan

during and after the war, see Ogata Toketoshi, comp., *Shisei gojūnen Taiwan sōsō shi* (The history of the inauguration of Taiwan's initial fifty years of rule) (Taihoku, 1944), pp. 183-84.

14. Hung Ch'i-sheng, p. 2.

15. These disturbances and the tense situation in Taiwan prior to the outbreak of the war are depicted in the accounts of western observers on the scene at the time. See Morse, letters 1290 (May 2, 1895) and 1298 (May 27, 1895); and Davidson's accounts printed in the *North-China Herald*, LIV, no. 1451 (May 24, 1895), 779.

16. Hung Ch'i-sheng, p. 5; and Hsieh Hsüeh-yü, "I-wei k'ang-Jih tsa-chi" (Miscellaneous records of the 1895 resistance against Japan), *T'ai-pei wen-wu*, IX, 1 (March, 1960), 74.

17. For example, when Japanese forces approached the town of Hsin-chu, the inhabitants prepared two sets of banners: one declaring themselves law-abiding subjects of Japan, and the other bearing words of welcome for the resistance forces. (Liu) Huang-ts'un, "Jih-chün ch'in Chu-i ch'ien-hou" (Account of the Japanese seizure of the town of Hsin-chu), *T'ai-pei wen-wu*, X, 2 (Sept., 1961), 110.

18. Accounts of disturbances indicating such mounting tensions may be found in Davidson's observations. See the *North-China Herald*, LIV, no. 1451, 779; and his book, *The Island of Formosa Past and Present*, pp. 268-74.

19. For example, members of the wealthy Lin Pen-yüan family assisted the Japanese in keeping peace in the Pan-ch'iao area. Sheng Ch'ing-i, "I-wei i-shang T'ai-pei shih-shih ts'ung-k'ao (Collection of investigations into the historical affairs of Taipei prior to 1895), *T'ai-pei hsien wen-hsien ts'ung-chi*, No. 1 (Sept., 1953), p. 86.

20. The slaughter of the Kwangtung troops is briefly dealt with in Wu Te-kung, pp. 41, 42-3; and the action against the Hakkas in Hsieh Hsüeh-yü, p. 79.

21. The discord between the intendant, Liu Ao, and Liu Ming-ch'uan during the French attack is discussed in

the biography of Liu Ao, contained in Lien Heng, pp. 697-98.

22. I have treated with T'ang Ching-sung and his efforts to remain the foremost resistance leader in Taiwan in an article entitled, "The 1895 Taiwan Republic: A Significant Episode in Modern Chinese History," *The Journal of Asian Studies,* XXVII, 4 (August, 1968), especially pp. 742-54.

23. *SLHC,* II, 264 (KH20/6/22).

24. *Ibid.,* 265 (KH20/6/27).

25. T'ang's activities during the period of the Sino-French War are dealt with in his diary: T'ang Ching-sung, *Ch'ing ying jih-chi* (Taipei, 1893). The circumstances involving his appointment as acting governor are mentioned in *SLHC,* II, 274-76 (KH20/9/12, 15, 25).

26. Yang and Lin showed their lack of confidence in T'ang by departing from Taiwan in May just before or after the rise of the republic. Ssu-t'ung tzu, *T'ai-hai ssu-t'ung lu* (Aggrieved report of the Taiwan sea) (Taipei, 1959, reprint), pp. 5-6. The ill will between T'ang and Liu is treated in Lo Hsiang-lin, ed., *Liu Yung-fu li-shih ts'ao* (Draft history of Liu Yung-fu) (Taipei, 1957, reprint), pp. 238-40.

27. Yao Hsi-kuang, *Tung-fang ping-shih chi-lüeh* (General account of eastern military affairs), first chapter, entitled "T'ai-wan p'ien," appended to Ssu-t'ung tzu, pp. 46-7.

28. Davidson, p. 286.

29. Previously, T'ang had attempted to secure funds through Hong Kong and Canton bank loans and by issuing bonds for sale to local merchants. In February he was granted a million taels by the Board of Revenue, based on a forced loan from Lin Wei-yüan. Chang Chih-tung was authorized to handle the funds and allot supplies to Taiwan. Morse, III, letter 1267 (March 2, 1895); and Tseng Nai-shih, "Chang Chih-tung yü T'ai-wan i-wei k'ang-Jih chih kuan-hsi" (The relation of Chang Chih-tung and the Taiwan resistance to Japan in 1895), *T'ai-wan wen-hsien,* X, 2 (June, 1959), pp. 26-7 (KH20/1/29).

30. For a brief account of their schemes and efforts to attract the aid of various western powers, see Wang Yün-

sheng, *Liu-shih-nien lai Chung-kuo yü Jih-pen* (China and Japan in the last sixty years) (Tientsin, 1932-1934), *chüan* 3, 28-36.

31. See the message T'ang telegraphed to Chang Chih-tung on May 17, contained in Tseng Nai-shih, p. 33 (KH21/4/23).

32. Lamley, "The 1895 Taiwan Republic: A Significant Episode in Modern Chinese History," pp. 742-48, 752-54.

33. T'ang failed to give the local gentry any real power under the republic. He also antagonized those in northern Taiwan by sending Lin Ch'ao-tung's mid-island volunteers back to the Taichung area instead of keeping these experienced troops posted at the strategic ridge to the west of Keelung where they had beat off a French attack ten years before. Yü Ming-chen, *T'ai-wan pa-jih chi* (Eight-day record of Taiwan), contained in the above cited work, *Ke T'ai san-chi*, p. 12.

34. Besides Lin and Admiral Yang, other important functionaries involved in defense matters who left at this time included the acting provincial treasurer and the Taipei prefect. Morse, III, letter 1298.

35. Hung Ch'i-sheng, p. 4; Lo Hsiang-lin, p. 240.

36. Ch'iu Jui-chia, "Hsien-hsiung Ts'ang-hai hsing-chuang" (Deportment of a deceased elder brother, Ts'ang-hai), reprinted in *T'ai-wan feng-wu*, IX, 4 (Oct. 1959), 39.

37. *SLHC*, II, 279 (KH20/11/1).

38. Ch'iu Ts'ung, "Ts'ang-hai hsien-sheng Ch'iu kung Feng-chia nien-p'u" (Nien-p'u of Ch'iu Feng-chia, Mr. Ts'ang-hai), reprinted in *T'ai-wan feng-wu*, IX, 4 (Oct., 1959), 46.

39. Late in March, Ch'iu planned to change his military seal to that of "Commander of the *i-chün* of each route (*lu*)," a title which indicates he wished to have control over such forces in all areas of Taiwan, particularly those in the north. However, by mid-April Ch'iu complained that he no longer exercised authority in the north. Ch'iu Lin, comp., "Ch'iu Feng-chia hsin-kao" (Drafts of Ch'iu Feng-chia's letters), *Chin-tai-shih tzu-liao*, 3 (June, 1958), 37 (KH21/3/3), and 41 (KH21/3/20).

40. *Ibid.*, 44 (KH21/4/21).

41. *North-China Herald,* LIV, no. 1451, 779. Here Ch'iu is referred to as the "Hakka chief, Ku Hung-kuk."

42. Yao Hsi-kuang, p. 48.

43. Eventually, on May 16, a confrontation between T'ang and Ch'iu took place. Ch'iu and a delegation of mid-island gentry made demands that indicate Ch'iu was at that time possibly the most influential leader on the island. Morse, III, letter 1298.

44. Tseng Nai-shih, "I-wei chih i Ch'iu Feng-chia shih-chi k'ao-cheng" (Investigation of traces of Ch'iu Feng-chia during the 1895 war), *T'ai-wan wen-hsien,* VII, 3-4 (Dec., 1956), pp. 65-69.

45. Some of these Hakka leaders, such as Ch'iu Kuo-lin, Chiang Shao-tsu, and Wu Hsiang, were killed in battle, and have been treated as martyrs in Taiwan history. Ch'iu Jui-chia, p. 39. For Ch'iu Feng-chia's rather high opinion of these leaders, most of them young gentry, see his letter of April 14, in Ch'iu Lin, p. 48 (KH21/3/20).

46. Lo Hsiang-lin, pp. 238-40.

47. Wu Te-Kung, p. 51. Eventually, local southern delegates appeared before Liu and implored him to become the new president of the republic. Liu spurned such requests. Lo Hsiang-lin, p. 248.

48. The intendant reportedly did not get along well with Liu. His leaving gave Liu full control over financial matters and the regular armed forces remaining in the southern region. Wu Te-kung, p. 50.

49. For comments on this parliament and an account of the issuance of stamps and currency in Tainan, see Wu Chih-ch'ing, "Tai-wan chan-cheng chi" (Record of the Taiwan war), *Chin-tai-shih tzu-liao,* 3 (1962), pp. 91-92. These remarks are contained in Wu's diary of events he witnessed while serving under Liu in Tainan.

50. Davidson, p. 325.

51. For details of Liu's narrow escape from the Japanese, see Lo Hsiang-lin, pp. 262-69.

52. Only in 1894 did Taipei gain official recognition as

the permanent provincial capital after work was suspended on the new capital site in the Taichung vicinity. *SLHC*, II, 257 (KH20/2/30).

53. This army seems to have been named after the semi-modern Ch'u army. It was modeled after a revised form of regulations for the Hsiang and Ch'u armies, and officers from the latter force served in it. Ssu-t'ung tzu, p. 12; Wu Te-kung, p. 47.

54. Wu Te-kung, p. 57.

55. Contemporaries of the period often allude to the way in which Liu intimidated the wealthy. See, for example, Hsieh Hsüeh-yü, p. 79; and Wu Te-kung, p. 70.

56. Wu Te-kung, pp. 47, 51; Ssu-t'ung tzu, p. 12.

57. Wu Te-kung, p. 34.

58. On the whole, relations between Li and the bureau managers were not harmonious. The local gentry objected to the prefect's deployment of the Hsin Ch'u Army in the Hsinchu district outside the bounds of the mid-island prefecture. In the latter part of July, the bureau managers petitioned Liu Yung-fu to send reinforcements to Chang-hua. They did so on their own initiative. *Ibid.*, p. 52.

59. This gentry figure was the Tainan *chin-shih,* Hsü Nan-ying, who commanded that city's *t'uan-lien* force as well. For glimpses of Hsü's activities during the war and his escape to the mainland after Liu Yung-fu had fled, see Hsieh Hsüeh-yü, pp. 75-6, 79.

60. The Japanese expedition sent to Taiwan in 1874 led to renewed use of the *pao-chia* system on the island. Then for the first time a prefectural bureau and sub-bureaus were organized to implement the various functions of the system. At the same time *t'uan-lien* bureaus and branches under official supervision made their appearance on the island with the head bureau also located in Tainan-fu. *T'ung-chih kao, chüan* 3, *Cheng-shih chih*; *Pao-an p'ien,* pp. 133, 147.

61. *Ibid.*, p. 171. In 1884, the Taiwan intendant, Liu Ao, first had organized a *yü-t'uan* force in Tainan during the French attack. His detailed regulations for such a protective sea force are contained in *Ibid.*, pp. 158-69.

62. The *t'uan-lien* battalions were often criticized for their allegedly padded rolls which enabled greedy gentry sponsors to pocket some of the funds allocated to these corps by the local authorities. *Ibid.*, p. 147.

63. Wu Te-kung, pp. 62-63.

64. Hsieh Hsüeh-yü. pp. 76, 79; Wu Te-kung, p. 51.

65. Some of these village efforts were carried out under local gentry leadership. See, for instance, Hung Ch'i-sheng, p. 12.

66. Wu Te-kung, pp. 55, 62-63.

67. Wu Chih-ch'ing, pp. 94, 103.

68. Li Ching-sung sent the Hsin Ch'u Army north into the Hsin-chu district early in July. Wu Te-kung, pp. 47-49, 53. Later in the same month Liu Yung-fu ordered two Black Flag battalions north to the mid-island districts. In charge of these units he placed his trusted aide, Wu P'eng-nien, who was subsequently killed in the battle of Pa-kua Mountain, mentioned below. *Ibid.*, pp. 53, 57; and I Shun-ting, *Hun nan chi* (Taipei, 1965, reprint), pp. 7-8.

69. Appeals addressed to Chang from both Li and Liu are to be found in Tseng Nai-shih, "Chang Chih-tung yü T'ai-wan i-wei k'ang-Jih chih kuan-hsi," pp. 38-39. In addition, Li and Liu sent representatives to the mainland to solicit aid from Chang and other officials in central and southern China. Wu Te-kung, p. 52; I Shun-ting, pp. 7-16.

70. Wu Te-kung, pp. 52-53, 55.

71. Ch'en Han-kuang, *T'ai-wan k'ang-Jih shih,* pp. 133, 146-47. The Chang-hua gentry managers even requested relief rations from the *pao-chia* bureau in Chia-i. Wu Te-kung, p. 55.

72. The district seats of both Chia-i and Hsin-chu witnessed a buildup of local volunteer and partisan forces. It is noteworthy that the Hakka partisans from Miao-li, led by Wu T'ang-hsing, did not receive a warm welcome in Hsin-chu when they demanded funds and supplies so that they might defend the town against the Japanese. Hung Ch'i-sheng, pp. 6-7.

73. Ssu-t'ung tzu, pp. 2-3.

74. See Yü Ming-chen's account of the short struggle for northern Taiwan in his *T'ai-wan pa-jih chi.* Also the observations of Davidson indicate the poor caliber of the troops and their commanders in the north during the war. Davidson, pp. 295-99.

75. Yü Ming-chen, p. 12.

76. Davidson, pp. 300-12.

77. *Ibid.*, pp. 300-304.

78. Ch'en Han-kuang, pp. 77-78; Hung Ch'i-sheng, pp. 4-5.

79. Sugiyama Seiken, pp. 28-29; Davidson, p. 312.

80. Ch'en Han-kuang, pp. 97-98.

81. *Ibid.*, p. 96; Davidson, p. 354.

82. Davidson, pp. 324-25, 353.

83. Hung Ch'i-sheng, p. 6.

84. Ch'en Han-kuang, pp. 98-99, 127-28; Wu Te-kung, pp. 54-55.

85. Ssu-t'ung tzu, p. 12.

86. Wu Te-kung, pp. 48-49, 52-55.

87. For details concerning Wu T'ang-hsing and his forces see Ch'en Han-kuang, pp. 78-80, and 174-75 (Wu's biography). Also, Wu Te-kung, pp. 42-43, 51-52.

88. Ch'iu Feng-chia introduced Wu to T'ang Ching-sung, and the latter is said to have given him the title "Commander of the Taiwan *i-min.*" Later on, Wu used a seal bearing such a title. Tseng Nai-shih, "Wu T'ang-hsing shih-chi k'ao-cheng" (Verification of the traces of matters pertaining to Wu T'ang-hsing), *T'ai-wan wen-hsien,* IX, 3 (Sept., 1958), 45, 49-50.

89. Wu Chih-ch'ing, p. 93.

90. Davidson, pp. 331-32; Ch'en Han-kuang, pp. 116-18.

91. Ch'en Han-kuang, p. 121.

92. This battle has been described by a number of writers. For the battle itself, see Davidson, pp. 336-39; for details concerning the fall of Chang-hua and Lu-kang, see Wu Te-kung, pp. 59-62.

93. Ch'en Han-kuang, pp. 130-34.

94. Part of the reason for the Japanese delay in Chang-hua stems from the epidemics of malaria and other diseases that incapacitated a sizable portion of the Imperial Guards. Davidson, pp. 339-41, 358.

95. *Ibid.*, pp. 353-54.

96. *Ibid.*, pp. 358-59; Ch'en Han-kuang, pp. 143-47; Sigiura Wasaku, p. 91.

97. Davidson, pp. 359-61.

98. *Ibid.*, pp. 354-56.

99. Davidson claims there were only about 4,000 "original" Black Flag troops under Liu's command. *Ibid.*, p. 353. This figure is cited here to suggest what the Black Flag strength seems to have been by the end of the summer. Only six Black Flag battalions were brought to Taiwan in 1894 when Liu was ordered to duty there. Lo Hsiang-lin, p. 236. Liu apparently recruited some Taiwan troops for his force after his arrival. From the troop listings in Ch'en Han-kuang (pp. 133-34) there would appear to have been at least a dozen battalions of Black Flag troops.

100. Davidson, pp. 357-58.

101. Hsieh Hsüeh-yü, pp. 75-76, 77.

102. See Kabayama's proclamation, dated October 27, 1895, addressed to the inhabitants of Tainan. Wakumoto Otokichi, comp., *Nisshin-eki Taiwan shi* (History of Taiwan in the Sino-Japanese War) (Taihoku, 1930), pp. 177-78. Later, on November 18, after it seemed that control had been gained over the southern Heng-ch'un district, the Governor-General issued a more formal pacification announcement. Sugiyama Seiken, p. 27.

103. Details as to such resistance, including the activities of so-called partisan patriots on the island over the next seven years, may be found in *T'ung-chih kao, chüan* 9, *Ke-ming chih; K'ang-Jih p'ien* (Records on revolution; Section on resistance to the Japanese) (Taipei, 1954), pp. 28-78.

104. *Ibid.*, p. 78; Ch'en Han-kuang, p. 165.

105. In mid-May the Peking authorities clearly showed their determination to have nothing more to do with the affairs of Taiwan. Then the representatives from the island,

sent to Peking to protest the cession of Taiwan, were "practically kicked out of the heavenly city," according to the *North-China Herald*, LIV, no. 1450, 741 (May 17, 1895). After that, the Peking government consistently forbade shipments of troops, arms, and supplies from the mainland to the island. (See note 2, above.) This official policy deterred authorities elsewhere in China from sending help to Taiwan during the war. There is much evidence against such assertions as that made by Davidson: "Every month Chang Chih-tung forwarded money, men, and arms in considerable quantity to Liu." Davidson, p. 351. See, for example, I Shun-ting, p. 15.

106. To westerners who arrived in Taiwan during the late Ch'ing period the settled areas of the island seemed a monotonous repetition of what they had seen in Fukien and Kwangtung. A. R. Colquhoun and J. H. Stewart-Lockhart, "A Sketch of Formosa," *The China Review*, XIII, 3 (Nov., 1884), esp. pp. 196-200.

107. Wu T'ang-hsing played upon the fear of living under the Japanese when attempting to recruit local villagers for his partisan band. As "slaves of the Dwarfs," he argued, all fields and property, as well as each person and every chicken, dog, ox and pig would be taxed, while everyone would have to wear different clothes and speak a strange language. Wu's announcement is cited in Ch'en Han-kuang, p. 80.

108. Ch'iu's efforts to appeal to the authorities on the mainland by alluding to the resentment of the Taiwan "gentry and people" may be seen in his well-known "petition written in blood." This was contained in a telegram T'ang sent to Peking on April 28. Pei-p'ing Ku-kuan po-wu-yüan (Peiping Palace Museum), comp., *Ch'ing Kuang-hsü ch'ao Chung-Jih chiao-she shih-liao* (Historical sources of the Sino-Japanese negotiations during the Kuang-hsü reign of the Ch'ing dynasty) (Taipei, 1963, reprint), I, 768, doc. 3038 (KH21/4/4).

109. For instance, see T'ang's message to Chang Chih-tung, dated May 20, contained in Tseng Nai-shih, "Chang

Chih-tung yü T'ai-wan i-wei k'ang-Jih chih kuan-hsi," p. 33 (KH21/4/26).

110. Recently, writers have tended more to emphasize the limited nature of China's foreign wars during the nineteenth century. For example, Ralph L. Powell, *The Rise of Chinese Military Power, 1895-1912* (Princeton, 1955), esp. p. 47.

111. Davidson, pp. 209-10, 213. Actually, such guns were first installed in 1880, but had been purchased the previous year in response to an alleged Russian threat.

112. Several recent works have dealt briefly with the construction of armament plants and a railroad in Taiwan in the light of late Ch'ing industrialization. In regard to Taiwan's arsenal and powder mill, see Wang Erh-min, *Ch'ing-chi ping-kung-yeh ti hsing-ch'i* (The rise of war industries during the late Ch'ing period) (Taipei, 1963), p. 120. In reference to railroad building see Li Kuo-ch'i, *Chung-kuo tsao-ch'i ti t'ieh-lu ching-ying* (China's early railroad enterprise) (Taipei, 1961), pp. 57-74.

113. A description of the weapons, new and old, used by the defenders of Taiwan is contained in Davidson, pp. 286-89.

114. *T'ung-chih kao, chüan* 3, *Cheng-shih chih; fang-shu p'ien,* p. 166.

115. The *pao-chia* system was authorized for use in Taiwan as early as 1733, and used infrequently on the island thereafter. *T'ung-chih kao, chüan* 3, *Cheng-shih chih; Pao-an p'ien,* p. 138, *passim. I-min* bands were active in Taiwan at least by the latter part of the eighteenth century when such forces operated during the Lin Shuang-wen uprising. See Huang Tien-ch'uan's most recent article on this subject, entitled, "Ch'ing Lin Shuang-wen chih pien chung ti i-min shou-ch'eng" (A partisan leader's insignia during the Lin Shuang-wen uprising of the Ch'ing period), *T'ai-wan feng-wu,* XVI, 3 (June, 1966), 27-30.

116. A number of such bureaus (*chü*) were formed in Taiwan, mostly after 1875, to handle new matters and emergency issues that arose. This same development is ap-

parent in other of China's provinces during the latter half of the nineteenth and early twentieth centuries, at least up to the time of the 1911 Revolution. A description of some of the more important "special offices" established in Taiwan is to be found in *T'ung-chih kao, chüan* 3, *Cheng-shih chih; Hsing-cheng p'ien* (Record of political affairs; Section on administration) (Taipei, 1957), pp. 209-14.

Glossary

An-p'ing	安平
Ao-ti	澳底
Chang-hua	彰化
Chia-i	嘉義
Chiang Shao-tsu	姜紹祖
Ch'iu Feng-chia	邱逢甲
Ch'iu Kuo-lin	邱國霖
ch'ou-fang chü	籌防局
Ch'u	楚
doki sōzoku	土匪草賊
Fang-liao	枋寮
Feng-shan	鳳山
Heng-ch'un	恒春
Hsiang	湘
Hsin-chu	新竹
Hsin-Ch'u (Army)	新楚
Hsü Hsiang	徐驤
Hsü Nan-ying	許南英
Huai	淮
i-chün	義軍
I-lan	宜蘭
i-min	義民
i-yüan	議院
i-yung	義勇
Kabayama Sukenori	樺山資紀
Li Ching-sung	黎景嵩
lien-chia chü	聯甲局
lien-chuang chü	聯(連)庄局
lien-yung	練勇
Lin Chan-mei	林占梅
Lin Ch'ao-tung	林朝棟
Lin Pen-yüan	林本源
Lin Wei-yüan	林維源
Liu Ao	劉璈
Liu Ming-ch'uan	劉銘傳
Liu Yung-fu	劉永福
Lo-tung	羅東
Lu-kang	鹿港
Miao-li	苗栗
Pa-kua (Mountain)	八卦
Pan-ch'iao	板橋
pao-chia	保甲
Pu-tai	布袋
Shao Yu-lien	邵友濂
Takao	打狗
Tainan-fu	台南府
Tan-shui	淡水
T'ang Ching-sung	唐景崧
Tou-liu	斗六
t'uan-fang	團防
t'uan-lien	團練
Tung-kang	東港
t'ung-ling	統領
Wu P'eng-nien	吳彭年
Wu T'ang-hsing	吳湯興
Yang Ch'i-chen	楊岐珍
Yang Ju-i	楊汝翼
ying	營
yü-t'uan	漁團
Yün-lin	雲林

Late Nineteenth Century Land Tenure in North Taiwan

EDGAR B. WICKBERG

Despite the importance of land tenure problems in recent decades, there has been little historical study of land tenure in Modern China. In large part this is due to limitations in available source materials. Until the rural surveys of the 1920s and 1930s, there was little systematic data collection about land conditions. One finds scattered references in various publications, and individual land documents occasionally turn up in libraries; but there have been few efforts to collate this material.[1]

In particular, detailed, accurate records, such as those resulting from cadastral surveys, are, on the whole, missing. There are, however, two major exceptions—the land records of Taiwan and those of the New Territories in Hong Kong. In both areas, the establishment of colonial regimes about 1900 resulted in cadastral surveys and in

EDGAR B. WICKBERG is Professor of History at the University of British Columbia and the author of *The Chinese in Philippine Life, 1850-1898* (New Haven: Yale University Press, 1965). His current paper regarding land tenure in northern Taiwan is part of a larger study of economic and social change in rural Taiwan since 1860. The author wishes to express his appreciation to Lin Hsin-hsiung for rendering research assistance.

conditions favorable to the orderly maintenance of land records.

This paper is a preliminary research report based mainly upon an analysis of the Taiwan land survey that was made by the Japanese between 1898 and 1903. Because this survey was carried out so soon after the Japanese occupation began, its results may be said to represent, in a general way, the land tenure situation in Taiwan as it was under Chinese rule in the last decades of the nineteenth century. These results may therefore add to our knowledge about land tenure in late Ch'ing China.

Because of the enormous quantity of records remaining from the Taiwan survey, it was necessary to limit the present analysis in some way. After considerable research, twelve villages[2] in three counties in North Taiwan were chosen. The North was selected because the records were most complete for that region and because it was the part of the Island most directly subjected to modernizing influences. Since this analysis of the 1898–1903 data is part of a larger study of the effects of modernization upon land tenure and rural society in Taiwan, the North, as the point of diffusion of modernizing influences, seemed particularly of interest.

In choosing villages for study, some attention was given to location and population density.[3] The major consideration, however, was the type of economic life. Thus, the twelve villages selected are intended generally to represent four types of local economy characteristic of North Taiwan in the late nineteenth century: subsistence rice production; small-scale tea cultivation mixed with rice production; surplus, market-oriented rice production; and large-scale tea cultivation.

If we take a family holding of about 1 hectare as a minimum subsistence size for late nineteenth century Taiwan,[4] we can establish, for working purposes, three categories of land holdings: small holdings of less than 2 hectares; medium-sized holdings of 2 to 10 hectares; and large holdings of over 10 hectares.

Let us first describe the ordinary, subsistence rice-producing village. Such villages, like those of South China in general, were populous. There might be 1,500 people per village, supported by about 300 hectares of village land. The average holding possible per family would thus be about 1 hectare of village land, or just about the minimum subsistence size for Taiwan at that time.[5] On the whole, land was widely distributed. In an average village, perhaps only one or two families might own as much as 10 hectares. At the other extreme, over 40% of the lands were in small holdings of less than 2 hectares. In between, about 50% of the lands were in moderate-sized holdings of 2 to 10 hectares.

In terms of land (our records are by land and not by families) tenancy was high. Perhaps as much as 75% of the land was tenant-cultivated. However, the majority of the owners of tenant-cultivated lands were themselves residents of the village. In these villages cultivated lands were planted mostly in rice, and those lands that were tenant-cultivated were almost all rice-producing lands. In general, two-thirds of the land in such a village was owned by individual families. Another 20% was jointly owned by several persons, most often brothers and cousins. The remaining 15% was corporately owned, primarily by kinship groups (*tsu*).

The characteristic form of ownership was that widely found in southeastern China and sometimes called "one-field, two-owners."[6] Originally, patents to open these lands had been given by the local government. Patent-holders had then recruited other people to do the work. In time, those who actually opened the lands had acquired rights of ownership which included the right to use the lands in any way they wished, to lease or encumber the lands, or even to sell them. The patent-holder and his heirs retained only the right to collect a certain income from each year's crop. These rights of patent-holder and owner were called, respectively, the *ta-tsu* ("big rent") and *hsiao-tsu* ("little rent") rights. Besides the kind of *ta-tsu* right just described there was another kind, held by the aborigines of Taiwan who, when they transferred some of their lands to the Chinese, retained a right to receive income, which was called *fan ta-tsu.* Thus, the majority of lands in these North Taiwan villages were subject to *ta-tsu*—sometimes payable to aborigines, depending on the location of the village. The amount of *ta-tsu* varied, but an average amount might be about 10% of the annual crop.[7] Until the 1880s, the land tax was paid by the patent-holder or holder of the *ta-tsu* right. Thereafter, the owner paid. It was payable only in cash, the rate being based upon the fertility and location of the land.[8]

If the owner of the land leased it to a tenant, he collected from the latter rent, or *hsiao-tsu.* The amount of rent varied with the kind of cultivation, the varying inputs of owner and tenant into the production process, and so forth. On paddy land, where tenancy was most common, it lay between 40 and 60% of the crop, most often paid in grain. Although written contracts existed, oral contracts apparently were the rule in North Taiwan and were usually on a three-to-five-year basis. In earlier times tenures had often been extended informally far beyond the contract term. However, in the late nineteenth century this practice broke down. As economic growth and population pressure increased land values, owners often shifted tenants with the expiration of each contract, in order to gain better terms.

This short-term tenure was only one of the tenant's

difficulties. The practice of demanding a substantial deposit in advance of the period of tenure was deeply rooted. Moreover, the *ta-tsu* and the costs of water rent were commonly passed on to the tenant. Buildings were furnished by the owner, but tools, seeds, and animals were usually the tenant's responsibility, as were labor costs. Thus, while tenants reportedly could barely meet their subsistence needs, rental incomes had doubled since the 1870s, and the *hsiao-tsu* right in 1900 could be sold for three times its price in the 1850s.[9]

In considering the small-scale tea village, it is necessary to note first that the economy of such villages was only partly based upon tea production. While approximately 25% of the village's land might be in tea, about 50% remained in rice. These small-scale tea villages were found in hilly regions, where terracing on hillsides for tea or rice cultivation was necessary. They were usually more populous than those just described but often had somewhat more land. In general, holdings were larger in such villages. The average owner-family had more land, and the percentage of small holdings was less. Very few people, however, owned over 10 hectares. Three-quarters of the land was tenant-cultivated, but more than half of the tenanted lands were absentee-owned. Both rice and tea lands were absentee-owned, rice more often than tea. Concerning the types of ownership, we find that in a small-scale tea village, as in an ordinary rice village, almost two-thirds of the land was individually owned; but in these tea villages there was more jointly-owned land and less corporately-owned land.

A third village type, the highly productive, market-oriented rice village, was one located on fertile soil, near an urban center, and with ready access to means of irrigation and transportation. Besides rice, it might also produce vegetables, which, like the rice, it could send to supply urban centers or other rural areas. The locational and economic advantages of these villages made land ownership in them more desirable than elsewhere. Outsiders would be interested in owning such lands. Because of the fertility and other advantages, however, the villagers themselves were more likely here than elsewhere to become prosperous and eager to invest in more lands.[10] The value of land in such places went up accordingly.

Holdings were larger than in villages already described. The average family holding might be about 2 hectares, and more than 70% of the lands in the village were in holdings larger than that. Again, 75% of the land was worked by tenants, and here about 85% of the village's lands were absentee-owned, reflecting perhaps the proximity of these villages to urban sources of investment or the transfer of residence by prosperous farmers from the village to a nearby town. It is worth noting that in some of these highly productive rice villages the two major landlord families of North Taiwan, the Lin of Pan-ch'iao and the Cheng of Hsin-chu, were among the largest holders.[11] Joint ownership in such villages, it can be observed, was more common than in small-scale tea villages. Both individual ownership and corporate ownership were relatively less important.

The fourth kind of village, the large-scale tea village, was located on the Taoyuan Plateau, where large contiguous amounts of land could be used for tea culture. Terracing in small plots was thus unnecessary. Here, land was available in relative abundance. The average family could have held about 2 hectares, but ownership of the land was less broadly distributed than that of the highly productive rice village. The average holding was in fact about 6 hectares. Land was often in tea estates, sometimes running into the hundreds of hectares. Over 80% of the land was in tea, and rice sometimes had to be imported for subsistence.[12] Typically, most of the land in one of these villages would be owned by a few families. In one instance a sinicized aboriginal family settled in the village was the major owner. In another, most of the land was owned by three of the richest town-dwelling families of North Taiwan.[13]

The rate of tenancy was about that found in other kinds of villages: 75%. As suggested above, sometimes the owners of tenanted lands were residents, sometimes they were absentees. There is no clear pattern visible among the villages studied except that absentee ownership was high.

Joint ownership was even more prominent in large-scale tea villages than in highly productive rice villages. It was, in fact, as common as individual ownership; and in such villages, corporate ownership was almost nonexistent.

If we survey our four village types across a spectrum from ordinary rice village, to small-scale tea village, to highly productive rice village, to large-scale tea village, we can see three general patterns. First, the size of holdings increases as one goes across this spectrum. In the ordinary rice village, the average family might own 1 hectare. The average increases until in the large-scale tea village the average holding might be, as indicated above, 6 hectares. The size of holdings may reflect demographic differences (although no pattern is readily visible). It certainly was affected by geographic factors and by differential economic abilities.

Second, although the situation in the large-scale tea villages is unclear, the other three parts of the spectrum show an increase in absentee ownership as one moves across from ordinary rice village to highly productive rice village. Tenancy in all villages amounted to about 75% of all cultivated lands. However, where most owners of tenanted lands in an ordinary rice village were themselves residents, the percentage of absentees increases as one goes across the spectrum. Except for the large-scale villages, absentee-owned lands were most likely to be rice lands. Thus, in the small-scale tea village one finds owner-producers on tea lands and tenants on absentee-owned rice lands. Perhaps those who took up tea culture sold to outsiders rice lands they no longer had time to cultivate.

Third, still looking across the same spectrum, there is an increase in joint ownership, while individual and corporate ownership decrease. In the large-scale tea villages, joint ownership, which accounted for 20% of the land in an ordinary rice village, had reached 50%. It is not yet clear whether this phenomenon merely reflects administrative convenience or chance, or, as it seems to be, is an indicator of familial or other group methods of retaining land of commercial value. Clearly, a closer examination of jointly held lands in each of the twelve villages and further study of patterns of inheritance will be necessary. In any case, it would appear that the three patterns here indicated are related to degrees of involvement in commercial agriculture. If so, then perhaps commercial agriculture, or at least surplus productivity, is related in Taiwan to larger holdings, absentee ownership (especially of rice lands), and the growth of joint ownership at the expense of other forms. The level of tenancy (75% everywhere) seems to have been unaffected. This uniformly high rate of tenancy may be related to population density,[14] or it may be the result of similar historical patterns of settlement in all the villages.

The Japanese survey was not the first made in North

Taiwan. In 1886, Governor Liu Ming-ch'uan initiated a partial survey. Most of the records of it have vanished, but fragments survive in the 1898-1903 materials and elsewhere, and some tentative comparisons are occasionally possible.[15] To the extent that we can compare, we find a general increase in the proportion of large holdings. This is particularly noticeable in the large-scale tea villages where tea landholdings over 10 hectares increased from about 50% of all lands to about 70%. It is also evident in one highly productive rice village, now a suburb of Taipei city, where holdings over 10 hectares increased from about 10% to almost 40%. Almost all these lands were in rice and vegetables, the surplus production of which was sent to the nearby city.

One may argue that these increases simply reflect more comprehensive measurement by the Japanese surveyors, and, indeed, the Japanese survey was more accurate and comprehensive. However, some of the increase must have been due to engrossment of holdings by owners.[16] It is worth repeating the fact of economic growth in the North. The continued growth of the tea trade, from the opening of the treaty ports in the 1860s to the end of the century, stimulated an extension of acreage under tea and a growing importance of land that could be used for tea cultivation. Population growth, and especially the urban development of Taipei, contributed to a general increase in the price of rice and in the value of lands suitable for rice and other foods. In this connection it may be noted that of the 12 villages studied the rice village just mentioned had, according to the Japanese survey, the largest holdings per owner and the highest rates of tenancy and absentee ownership.

We have said nothing yet about mortgages. In nineteenth-century Taiwan the characteristic mortgage-type arrangement was the pledge, or *tien*, which was widely used in China. In the *tien*, an owner of land borrowed money, pledging his land to the lender for the latter to use during the term of the loan. Instead of collecting interest, the lender had the use of the land as compensation until the loan was repaid. The *tien* had long been used in Taiwan, but in the late nineteenth century only about 6% of the lands in the villages studied were subject to this arrangement.[17]

This rather small percentage of *tien*-affected lands may indicate that the *tien* institution had become less important than before as a way of conveying property and perhaps as a vehicle for transfer of ownership. It appears from archives of the largest landowner in the North that that family usually acquired its lands in the late nineteenth century through outright purchase.[18] Probably this was the usual method in Taiwan without any involvement of *tien*.

The *ta-tsu* right, referred to above, was fading into nonexistence. Patent holders were increasingly unable to collect the *ta-tsu* owed to them. One reason was the decline of some patent-holding families. Another may have been a strengthening of the position of landowners due to the increase in land values. Still another must have been the reforms of Liu Ming-ch'uan, who ordered that beginning in 1889 the land tax in North Taiwan should be paid by the landowner rather than the *ta-tsu* holder. In order to compensate the former for his increased burden, he directed that the *ta-tsu* rent be reduced by 40%. The result was to make the *ta-tsu* right less important in the North and to put the landowner in a stronger position relative to the government than he had been earlier. Whatever the reasons, landowners simply ceased paying their *ta-tsu* rent or deferred payment indefinitely, and *ta-tsu* patent holders seemingly could do nothing to enforce their claims. Even the most powerful patent holders were increasingly failing to collect, even from small, weak landowners.[19]

In comparison with Mainland China at the same time, Taiwan's land tenure conditions appear rather like those in many parts of the rice-growing South. Holdings in Taiwan were somewhat larger. The rate of tenancy, however, was as high or higher in Taiwan, and rental rates in both places were about at the 50% level.

In terms of the history of land tenure in Taiwan, this analysis of 1898-1903 records indicates that tenancy rates were already very high when the Japanese took over the Island. Therefore, although the Japanese undoubtedly affected tenancy, the common argument that tenancy in Taiwan is a direct result of Japanese colonial policies seems to require revision.

Notes

1. For an early attempt to report on conditions in certain localities, see George Jamieson et al., "Tenure of Land in China and the Condition of the Rural Population," *Journal of the North China Branch, Royal Asiatic Society*, new series, XXIII (1888), pp. 59-174. Recently, further collecting and analyzing efforts have been made; for example: Li Wen-chih (comp.), *Chung-kuo chin-tai nung-yeh shih tzu-liao, ti-i chi, 1840-1911* [Historical materials on modern Chinese agriculture, first collection] (Peking, 1957); Amagai Kenzaburō, *Chūgoku tochi bunsho no kenkyū* [A study of Chinese land documents] (Tokyo, 1966); and several articles by Muramatsu Yūji in *Kindai Chūgoku kenkyū*, V (1963), pp. 1-184; *ibid.*, VI (1964), pp. 1-66; and elsewhere.

2. "Village" here refers to the administrative village, or *chuang*. The *chuang* was used for reasons of convenience in working with the records of the 1898-1903 survey.

3. The records of the 1898-1903 survey are found in Rinji Taiwan tochi chōsa kyoku, *Tochi shinkoku sho* [Land reports] (unpublished): Kung-kuan-hou chuang (San-hsia chen, Taipei hsien); Ting-chiao chuang (Chin-shan hsiang, Taipei hsien); Tan-li chuang (Kung-liao hsiang, Taipei hsien); Shan-tzu-ting chuang (P'ing-chen hsiang, Taoyuan hsien); Chih-t'an chuang (Hsin-tien chen, Taipei hsien); K'eng-tzu chuang (Lü-chu hsiang, Taoyuan hsien); Lun-tzu chuang (Hsin-chu city); T'ou-ch'ien chuang (Hsin-chuang chen, Taipei hsien); p'eng-fu chuang (Shu-lin chen, Taipei hsien); Fu-te-yang chuang (Shih-lin chen, Taipei hsien); Ta-an-liao chuang (T'u-ch'eng hsiang, Taipei hsien); T'ung-lo-ch'uan chuang (Lung-t'an hsiang, Taoyuan hsien). These

materials are in the custody of the Provincial Bureau of Lands, Taipei. I am indebted to Director Shen Shih-k'o for permission to use them. Note that the *hsiang/chen* and *hsien* names given above are the contemporary ones, not those of 1898-1903. Population, productivity, and land value statistics of use in choosing the 12 villages studied are found in *Taiwan genjū jinkō tōkei* [Current population statistics of Taiwan] (1905); *Den shūkaku satei sho* [Assessments of paddy harvests] (1905); *Den baibai kakaku oyobi kinri chōsa sho* [Investigations of market values and interest rates concerning paddy] (1905); *Hatake shūkaku satei sho* [Assessment of dry field harvests] (1905); *Hatake baibai kakaku oyobi kinri chōsa sho* [Investigations of market values and interest rates concerning dry fields] (1905).

4. Naturally, the amount of land needed for a family's subsistence varied with the quality of the land and the number of harvests possible. I follow examples given in Rinji Taiwan kyūkan chōsa kai, dai ni bu, *Keizai shiryō hōkoku* [Report on materials about the economy], 2 vols. (Tokyo, 1904), II, pp. 574-77.

5. For a discussion of the size of South China villages compared with those of North China, see Kung-ch'uan Hsiao, *Imperial China: Rural Control in the Nineteenth Century* (Seattle, 1960), pp. 12-19. In Taiwan the average size household in 1905 was 5.2 persons. George Barclay, *Colonial Development and Population in Taiwan* (Princeton, 1954), p. 175.

6. See Niida Noboru, *Chūgoku hōsei shi* [History of the legal system of China] (Tokyo, 1952), pp. 290-97; and Tai Yen-hui, "Ch'ing-tai Taiwan chih ta-hsiao-tsu yeh" [The 'ta-tsu' and 'hsiao-tsu' property rights in Taiwan in the Ch'ing period], *Taipei wen-hsien*, IV (June 1963), pp. 1-47.

7. Okamatsu Santarō et al. (comp.), *Provisional Report on Investigations of Laws and Customs in the Island of Formosa* (Kyoto, 1902?), p. 84. The *ta-tsu* obligation fell more upon rice lands than tea lands. Perhaps this reflects the fact that tea lands were often brought into cultivation only in the

middle and late nineteenth century when the *ta-tsu* right was losing its strength.

8. See Rinji Taiwan tochi chōsa kyoku (comp.), *Shin fu ippan* [General view of the Ch'ing land survey in Taiwan] (Taihoku, 1900), pp. 6-8, 61.

9. *Keizai shiryō hōkoku,* I, p. 27; II, p. 575; Shiro Kawada, "The Tenant System of Formosa," *Kyoto University Economic Review,* III, 2 (Dec. 1928), pp. 100, 104; Okamatsu, *Provisional Report,* pp. 26, 74, 85, 92, 94, 111-12, 115-18; Rinji Taiwan kyūkan chōsa kai, *Dai Nikai hōkoku* [Second report of the temporary commission on old customs], 5 vols. (Taihoku, 1906-1907), I, pp. 598-625. Tai, "Ch'ing-tai Taiwan chih ta-hsiao-tsu yeh," pp. 9, 11, 12; Lin Pen-yuan t'ang, ti-i-fang tang-an [Archives of the eldest branch, Lin Pen-yuan family] (Taipei). Land contracts. I am indebted to Lin Hsiung-hsiang for permission to examine these materials.

10. Hsiao, *Imperial China,* p. 384.

11. At least one-fourth of the land of one village was owned by 12 holders, three of whom were members of the Lin family of Pan-ch'iao.

12. Interviews at Kuan-hsi (June 1, 1966); Lung-t'an (June 1, 1966); T'ung-lo-ch'uan (May 25, 1966).

13. Interviews at Kuan-hsi, June 1, 1966.

14. There were 87 persons per square kilometer in Taiwan in 1905. Tang Hui-sun, *Land Reform in Free China* (Taipei, 1954), p. 12.

15. See *Shin fu ippan; Tochi shinkoku sho;* and Rinji Taiwan tochi chōsa kyoku, *Jigyō hōkoku,* dai ikkai [First project report on the land survey] (Taihoku, 1902), esp. pp. 158-201.

16. Archives of the largest landowner of North Taiwan indicate that that family steadily increased its land purchases during the period in question. Lin Pen-yuan t'ang, ti-i-fang tang-an. Land contracts.

17. *Tien* are described in Rinji Taiwan kyūkan chōsa kai, dai ichi bu, *Taiwan shihō* [Private law in Taiwan], 13 vols. (Taihoku, 1910-1911), I, pt. 1, pp. 651-710.

18. Lin Pen-yuan t'ang, ti-i-fang tang-an. Land contracts.

19. *Ibid.*, Account books, especially those of 1874, 1879, 1889, and 1895. Okamatsu, *Provisional Report*, pp. 74, 78.

Taiwan and the Powers, 1840–1895

LEONARD H. D. GORDON

The effort made by Chinese officials to develop Ch'ing institutions on Taiwan shortly before the Japanese occupation in 1895 was the product of an intense challenge to China's sovereign claim to the island. A viable political structure, a stable economy, and the Chinese social order were part of a broad program of sinification entrusted to Liu Ming-ch'uan when he was made the first Governor of Taiwan province in 1886.[1] This belated interest in Taiwan by the Chinese political hierarchy was a program of westernization, accepted reluctantly, to respond to more than four decades of pressuring by Western powers and Japan, or their representatives, to gain a foothold on the island. In the process Taiwan became a diplomatic pawn of international politics.

The series of diplomatic episodes between 1840 and 1895, while generally unrelated, form a pattern of de-

LEONARD H. D. GORDON is Associate Professor of History at Purdue University. He has published several articles on nineteenth-century Taiwan, including "Japan's Abortive Colonial Venture in Taiwan, 1874," *The Journal of Modern History*, XXXVII, 2 (June, 1965), pp. 171-85. The present article is the subject of a monographic study currently in progress.

velopment that reveals significant aspects of international policy in nineteenth-century East Asia, as well as China's xenophobic response to foreign encroachment. The pattern established by the major powers was one which required co-operation both among the countries having relations with China and in their collective approach toward China. Emphasis was on conciliation and protection for Chinese sovereignty over all territories for which China held a traditional claim.

The Co-operative Policy was not one which had been formally pronounced by the major powers. It was never given the strength and prominence of being a treaty stipulation. Rather, it was a policy implicit in the expressed attitudes of leading diplomats and given credence by their official deeds. The policy had a dual meaning. It was *co-operative* in the sense that the major powers, specifically Great Britain, the United States, Japan, and France, had a sort of "Gentlemen's Agreement" which, while it permitted them to extract commercial privileges from China, would not permit them the luxury of obtaining territorial concessions or allow others to do so. The aim of the policy was to maintain equal commercial opportunity for all interested powers. In this context the "Open Door" policy at the end of the nineteenth century was merely a reaffirmation of the Co-operative Policy at mid-century.

Another important aspect of the Co-operative Policy is the expressed desire to approach China in a conciliatory way, respecting China's sovereign rights as a nation, mindful of her sensitivities and cultural distinctiveness, and, above all, to condemn force as an instrument of diplomacy. As well-documented in the historical record, conciliatory behavior on the part of strong powers was frequently discarded in practice. But these episodes were more often caused by a breakdown in communications between officials at home and those in the field along the China coast rather than by established policy and design.

The concept of a Co-operative Policy as being a principal guide to the western approach to China in the nineteenth century has only in recent years been given recognition by historians.[2] Because of the confused quilt-work of major power diplomacy in China, frequently jarred by exceptions and reversals, the Co-operative Policy was either ignored or given heavily qualified support as a legitimate explanation for international events in East Asia during the last century. The example of Taiwan, however, illustrates the significant and effective role that the Co-operative Policy had in protecting Chinese territory from foreign seizure. In each major episode where external pressure was brought to bear against Taiwan between 1840 and 1895, direct interference by one or more major powers was responsible for preserving Taiwan as an integral part of China.

Another factor which must receive attention, however, is the Chinese response to this western-conceived policy. Basically, Chinese officialdom was adamant in preventing the loss of any territory. Despite internal weakness and disorder, Chinese officials argued vociferously and consistently that the sovereign rights China traditionally maintained over her territory could never be relinquished to another power. China's firm diplomatic stand on this principle, however, was virtually irrelevant when confronted with the challenge of superior military force. Her tortuous arguments attempting to substantiate China's claim to territory over which she had minimal political control received little sympathy from western legalists whose guide was Wheaton's *International Law*. The significant question of China's sovereignty rested in the hands of western diplomats who saw advantage in the maintenance of an independent and viable China.

The Co-operative Policy was thus not only a plan for the preservation of commercial opportunity but was equally significant as a scheme to preserve the territorial integrity of China. Each aspect was, of course, essential to the preservation of the other.

In viewing the problem of Taiwan as a "case study" in the Co-operative Policy, it may best be seen from its historical perspective. A brief survey of the series of episodes of major power encroachment upon Taiwan and the ramifications resulting from these episodes to China's claim over the island should illustrate the persistent role played by this policy.

The first countries that showed an interest in Taiwan were Great Britain and the United States. Their involvement with the island was hardly deliberate. It was in large measure due to the general search for greater commercial opportunity and coal resources along the China coast and the problems caused by shipwrecked mariners on Taiwan. The former interest was due to a greater scheme, the latter was due to accident.

An early clash over Taiwan came in 1841-1842. While Great Britain and China were engaged in conflict, two British ships foundered on the coast of southern Taiwan. The extreme measures of beheading the survivors of the wrecks by Chinese local authorities quite naturally caused great consternation at a time when British-Chinese relations were at their lowest ebb. Amid a torrent of charges and counter-charges, the incident was settled when British accusations that innocent castaways had been indiscriminately executed were sustained.[3] While the episode threatened the Treaty of Nanking and engendered severe embitterness between the participating factions, no infringement was made on China's sovereignty.

American attention was first drawn to Taiwan in the

mid-nineteenth century search for coaling stations and unconfirmed information that missing American ships may have foundered on the island's coast. This led to a series of search expeditions that resulted, first, in little positive information about the missing mariners and, second, knowledge of coal resources readily accessible on the northern coast but of dubious quality.[4]

The earliest occasion upon which an American registered an interest in territorial concession on Taiwan was made by Dr. Peter Parker, medical missionary and sometime diplomat, when in 1851 he initiated a search there for survivors rumored to be enslaved by aboriginal tribes. Before he became more grossly involved with Taiwan the subordinates of Commodore Matthew C. Perry made an investigation for coal resources and shipwrecked mariners during the interlude in his mission to Japan in the winter of 1853-1854.[5] Although Perry's officers found little more than what had already been known about these matters, he quickly became entranced with the island's potential and virtually advocated an American protectorate over it. He believed that "the United States alone should assume the initiative" in fostering improved political and civil conditions in Asia.[6] The advantages of an American-controlled Taiwan were numerous: an entrepôt for American trade, enhancement of the American naval and military position in East Asia, and an abundant source of coal for the steamers that carried the rapidly expanding American trade in East Asia.[7] In his persuasive efforts, Perry was strongly supported by Townsend Harris, then at Macao.[8]

The issue of coal resources and maritime survivors again came to Dr. Peter Parker's attention in 1857; and on this occasion, he firmly recommended that American commitment be made to establish its presence on Taiwan. Stirred by reports of possible mistreatment to American survivors on the island by native aborigines, he categorically declared that American action was essential "in the interests of humanity and commerce." Encouraged by willing compatriots who recommended colonization, he wrote to Washington that the United States should "not *shrink* from the *action* which the interests of humanity, civilization, navigation and commerce impose upon it."[9] Parker's enthusiasm for Taiwan mounted rapidly, and he justified temporary seizure of the island as a reprisal until reparations could be made for the injuries sustained by Americans by citing passages from Wheaton's *International Law.* He even considered entering into a coordinated effort with Great Britain and France to exert such pressure against China in areas of interest to each of them. The aim was to be a general expansion of "free and unrestricted commercial intercourse."[10] Without waiting for a decision from Washington, Parker attempted to interest the commander of the United States East India Squadron, Commodore James Armstrong, in his reprisal scheme and found him very sympathetic.[11]

Parker's cause for anxiety was a growing concern about a rumor emanating from Hong Kong that the British were also interested in Taiwan and might be scheming to seize it before the Americans. An exchange of correspondence between Parker and Sir John Bowring, British Plenipotentiary in Hong Kong,[12] confirmed Parker's fears but led to no action by either nation. While the American Secretary of State never answered Parker's proposals for the acquisition of Taiwan, he clearly forbade any aggressive measures against Chinese territory.[13] When the new Minister to China, William B. Reed, assumed office later in the same year, he quickly brought an end to Parker's expansionism and wrote candidly to his Secretary of State, Lewis Cass, that "Eastern colonization is not yet part of our policy, and it is as well not to be suspected of it."[14]

The British home government assumed the same posture. The policies of the major powers were clearly opposed to territorial seizure in China. Although subordinate representatives in China may have favored, proposed, and even schemed to promote a policy of aggrandizement, the official policy of their government scrupulously avoided granting either sanction or encouragement to them.

In the 1860s the Co-operative Policy became a conscious program for engaging in diplomatic relations with China. The development of the policy was seriously hindered by sharp differences of opinion between the home governments and their nationals in East Asia. This was most decidedly apparent in Great Britain. The root of the problem was to be found in the British mercantile community in China which erroneously believed that China's large population was a great potential market for British manufactured goods. In 1858 a report by a lower British official in Hong Kong, prepared six years earlier, had been discovered and belatedly forwarded to London where it had a tremendous impact. The pessimistic report of commercial potential in China, now substantiated by more recent trade statistics, prompted the British foreign office and the Board of Trade to adopt a more clearly defined policy of caution and conciliation[15] in which all the powers would work together in concert. It rested upon the realization that a strong and stable China was in the common interest of all the major powers.

The British, in fact, gave further dimension to the developing Co-operative Policy by attempting to buttress the Peking government against internal dissension. It did so by giving support to the maritime customs and sternly instructing its representatives to avoid placing pressure upon local authorities in seeking a redress of grievances and to bring such problems directly to Peking.[16] Despite these instructions, determined mercantilists continued to go their own way and repeatedly jeopardized the Co-operative Policy. It was given particular strength and some formalization, however, in a joint statement of Lord Clarendon, British foreign secretary, and Anson Burlingame, leader of a Chinese mission abroad, made in December of 1868. This "Clarendon Declaration," as it came to be known, emphasized the need for Europeans to work in concert and avoid placing any degree of unfriendly pressure on China, as well as to assure that country that British policy would follow this course; but the Declaration also stipulated that China's responsibility would require faithful observance of the treaties, a factor which was stressed by the policy-makers in London but overlooked by the merchants in China who quickly became supercritical of the "new" policy. The formalization of the Co-operative Policy and its contradiction by merchants—and even Consuls—in China is illustrated by events in Taiwan.

In the 1860s greater interest developed in Taiwan, because it was now legally opened to foreign trade as a result of the Treaty of Tientsin (1858). In the latter portion of this decade, two incidents involving the major proponents of the Co-operative Policy, the United States and Great Britain, illustrate both the continued conflict between the home governments and their nationals in East Asia and the real strength of that policy in guaranteeing the territorial integrity of China.

In 1867 an American shipwreck along the Taiwan coast stimulated the greatest American interest in the island to date. The American Consul at Amoy, Charles W. LeGendre, whose jurisdiction touched upon Taiwan, made his own personal investigation of the situation there, and at best only obtained a promise from the Chinese authorities on the island to send a military expedition to the troubled areas to make it secure for shipwrecked survivors.[17] At about the same time, the American Consul at Hong Kong, Isaac J. Allen, kindled the old fires regarding the acquisition of Taiwan. He felt that it would be "the greatest boon that our Government could confer upon our national commerce in the East."[18] This renewed enthusiasm for the seizure of Taiwan was once again met with calculated restraint by the American government. Secretary of State William H. Seward, despite his own vibrant interest in expanding American influence in the Pacific area, cautioned the American Minister in Peking in his instructions "that in no case do the United States desire to seize and hold possession of Formosa [Taiwan] or any part of said island."[19]

Apparently oblivious to the constraint from Washington, LeGendre made his own expedition against the aborigines in southern Taiwan with the help of the American naval squadron in the South China Sea. Despite the potential danger involved in a confrontation with the aborigines on Taiwan, LeGendre was able to come to a peaceful agreement with them whereby they offered guarantees that the earlier "outrages" would not be repeated against future survivors.[20] The firm measures taken by LeGendre in dealing with the Chinese officials on Taiwan came close to insubordination, yet they remained limited to an immediate redress of grievances rather than a permanent seizure of Chinese territory.

An even more direct affront to the Co-operative Policy occurred about the same time from British diplomats. While LeGendre was attempting to subdue the aborigines' passion for assault against shipwrecked mariners, general disturbances arose on Taiwan over the camphor monopoly and missionary activities. In two incidents in 1868, one at Meng-chia (near present-day Taipei) and Anping, the use of British military force threatened the Co-operative Policy and was responsible for a probing reappraisal of the conciliatory approach to China. In a dispute over camphor, a British trader was seized, but later escaped, in his effort to break the Chinese monopoly in this product. A British naval commander, as well as LeGendre who had been in the vicinity at the time, attempted to pressure the Chinese into abstaining from interference in the camphor trade of British merchants. Neither was successful.[21]

In addition to the camphor question, general friction between British residents and the local population had developed with respect to missionary activity. During April 1868, in the same month that the camphor problem had arisen, a Catholic and a Protestant chapel in Fengshan *hsien* were burned and sacked, and a catechist was murdered five miles from the British Consulate. Suspicions and false rumors about the activities of Christian missionaries enraged the already hostile populace, and violence resulted.[22] After a period of disturbances against British missionaries in Taiwan, British patience wore thin, and consideration was given to a military response. A show of force was not in accord with the Co-operative Policy, and missionary activity was rapidly becoming an irritant to British officialdom itself. Finally, resistance to a British merchant who sought to open a *hong* in Mengchia, in northern Taiwan, led to the British Acting Vice Consul, H. F. Holt, calling upon support from a British gunboat to threaten Chinese officials in the vicinity.[23] Before the situation exploded into conflict, LeGendre rendered his good offices, and a settlement satisfactory to the British demands was reached.

This series of disturbances, however, finally led to collusion between British Consuls and naval officers in the vicinity of Anping in southern Taiwan and the launching of a military expedition against the Chinese position at

Fort Zeelandia. In the settlement that took place following the engagement, the British extracted an indemnity from the Chinese to satisfy the demands of the foreign merchants. In the discussions that followed, Sir Rutherford Alcock, the British Minister in Peking, appeared to support the Co-operative Policy but in more frank remarks registered sympathy with the use of force.[24] There was considerable support for the latter sentiment among military and naval commanders and lower-ranking diplomatic officials, in addition to the mercantile community. Nevertheless, Lord Clarendon firmly reiterated the policy of conciliation and declared that those responsible for forceful action were wrong "to commit any acts of hostility whatever."[25]

The greatest threat to the Co-operative Policy of the 1860s came from Japan in 1874. In less than a year the Japanese had directed a military occupation of Taiwan, engaged in extensive diplomatic wrangling with Chinese and western diplomats, and stood on the brink of war with China. The entire Japanese effort was reversed by British pressure directed toward the maintenance of China's territorial integrity.

Japan's interest in the island was first stimulated by the loss of fifty-four Ryūkyūan sailors who were murdered by the aborigines there in 1871. The potential value of Taiwan was soon recognized by the Japanese. In the following year their interest was heightened by LeGendre's arrival in Japan. LeGendre was returning to the United States from his post in Amoy. Through the good offices of the American minister, Charles DeLong, LeGendre was hired as a specialist to advise the Japanese government on Taiwan affairs. In a series of lengthy memorandum and discussions with the Japanese Foreign Minister, Soeshima Taneomi, LeGendre fired the same enthusiasm for

Taiwan that he himself had exhibited earlier.[26] In advising the Japanese to take Taiwan, LeGendre outlined a plan of conquest in minute detail.[27]

In its effort to acquire Taiwan, however, Japan first engaged in diplomatic maneuvers. Accompanied by LeGendre, Soeshima went to China where they engaged in discussions in Tientsin and Peking. The Japanese strategy was to force the Chinese into admitting that they were unable to effect political administration in the portion of Taiwan occupied by the aborigines. Admission of this fact would acknowledge Japan's right to use force in subduing those aborigines responsible for the earlier disturbances. These conversations concluded in an ambiguous arrangement in which the Chinese nominally consented to allow Japan to send a "military mission" to Taiwan. The size of this mission, however, was never clarified. Soeshima finally recommended to his government that it use military force "to take this land and make it a Japanese possession and the southern gate of the empire.[28]

By the spring of 1874 a sufficient number of Japanese officials favored taking a firm stand on Taiwan and following LeGendre's advice to annex at least the aboriginal portion of the island. In March Saigō Tsugumichi, a samurai from Kagoshima, led a military expedition to southern Taiwan which was essentially a colonization scheme.[29] The entire operation was directed from Nagasaki, where a special agency was created to coordinate all aspects of the expedition.

Once the military operations were successfully completed in a few weeks and a base was developed on Taiwan, the diplomatic effort was resumed. After negotiations in China and on Taiwan failed to accomplish a settlement, and the two countries came near war, the Japanese government initiated high-level negotiations at Peking, led by Ōkubo Toshimichi. The stabilizing element in these conferences was the interference of British Minister John Wade. Negotiations had become snarled over the question of whether Chinese sovereignty extended to the aboriginal area of Taiwan in view of China's earlier disclaimer to effective administration there.[30] If the Chinese had held to this position, they would have left themselves open to the argument that China then had no right to interfere with Japan's mission to Taiwan.

Minister Wade worked diligently and directly to prevent a conflict between China and Japan and repeatedly urged a withdrawal of Japanese troops. When Ōkubo seemed obstinate in his refusal to concede to China's claim to the island, Wade did not hesitate to threaten the expansion of British naval strength in the vicinity of Taiwan.[31] This expression of force was not made in general hostility toward Japan but in accord with the Cooperative Policy to prevent any single power from attaining predominance in China. Both Ōkubo and LeGendre, however, were aware that the British were not anti-Japanese,[32] and they tended to take the British warnings lightly.

The Japanese, nevertheless, were adamant in their demands; and by early October the negotiations appeared to be near the breaking point. While earlier issues were settled and the Japanese were willing to withdraw from Taiwan, the question of an indemnity remained insoluble. In despair at being pressured to make concessions to China for a special settlement of the whole affair, Ōkubo announced his intention to leave Peking. LeGendre had already left. In a final effort to arrange a peace settlement, Wade, fearful of war, urged further discussions; and it was in these talks between him and Ōkubo that the final agreement was made.[33] The British Minister had clearly overseen every step of the negotiations and was primarily responsible for the final settlement. The territorial integrity of China was again maintained.

Another decade was to elapse before Taiwan became the object of further foreign aggrandizement. This time, the island had become a pawn in the conflict between France and China in 1884-1885. When France was unable to dislodge Chinese troops on the Indo-China-Yunnan border, she demanded an indemnity to compensate for her losses in the military skirmishes there. The Chinese refusal to pay caused France to seize the Pescadores and to exert military pressure against Taiwan, which in turn resulted in the siege of Keelung and Tamsui. The Chinese defenses on Taiwan, however, were capable of preventing surrender of the island to French forces, and a military stalemate between the two countries resulted.[34]

While Great Britain and the United States held firm to the Co-operative Policy, France vacillated. The Tientsin Massacre in 1870 had led France to assume a more aggressive and demanding attitude in her relations with China. At first the mercantile-minded elements in the treaty ports favored the French advance toward the southwestern provinces of China in the hope that the crisis might help to break down Chinese trade barriers. However, when the French undertook an occupation of a portion of Taiwan, fears were expressed that France might have territorial designs on China. The merchant community, which favored a policy that would further their own goals, as well as those of the diplomatic community, were now quick to react against the acquisition of exclusive rights by the French.[35]

When the French instituted a blockade of Taiwan in October, 1884 to put still more intensive pressure upon China, the major powers began to show their displeasure. Great Britain objected to France's claim to a "pacific blockade" in view of her large-scale hostilities in Taiwan, and she also raised objection to the French consideration of rice as a contraband of war.[36] In her observance of neutrality, Great Britain did so only to the extent that it did not prevent rendering advice and assistance to China. Other powers, such as Germany, sold military supplies and equipment to China. It was the Krupp guns that successfully contained the French forces in Keelung. Sympathy ran with China, and the French were well aware of it. When the United States offered mediation, France refused, fearing that any settlement to which the United States was a party would favor China.[37]

In her search for allies, France turned to Japan because of that nation's interest there a decade before. The French government reasoned that if it offered Taiwan to Japan as spoils of war, Japan would be willing to permit the use of its ports and to assist materially in Tonkin, which remained France's foremost interest.[38] After due consideration, the Japanese refused to become a part of the French scheme. By this time the Japanese leaders who earlier favored expansion in Taiwan were no longer in leadership positions and the nation was particularly desirous of maintaining good relations with China because of a delicate situation developing over Korea and the presence of Chinese and Japanese troops there. Thus, France found no allies and no sympathy for her Taiwan campaign. The effective military defenses in Taiwan and the successful Chinese counterattack on the Indo-China border, coupled with a hostile response from the major powers, led France to withdraw from Taiwan.

The last episode in which Taiwan was to become a subject of nineteenth-century diplomacy in East Asia occurred in 1894-1895 when the island became involved in the Sino-Japanese War. Although Japanese strategists gave some attention to Taiwan during the war, it did not become a fundamental question until the peace negotiations at Shimonoseki in the spring of 1895. When discussions reached an impasse over an armistice agreement, Prime Minister Itō Hirobumi informed Li Hung-chang, China's chief negotiator, that a Japanese expedition was preparing to leave for southern Taiwan. This Japanese effort at "gunboat diplomacy" did not frighten Li, who raised the specter of the threat to British interests because of Taiwan's proximity to Hong Kong. Itō, however, was unimpressed.[39]

Once the negotiations had been resumed, after the interruption caused by the attempted assassination of Li Hung-chang, the question of Taiwan became the primary obstacle to a peace settlement. Itō was adamant on acquiring Taiwan, and Li, though belatedly, was equally determined to prevent any cession of Chinese territory. He raised every conceivable argument possible in objecting to the Japanese demands. Finally on April 15th—significantly the day before the conclusion of the armistice period that was arranged when negotiations had been resumed—Li consented to relinquish Taiwan to Japan.[40]

Where were the major powers now and their Cooperative Policy? It had now become evident that the policy no longer existed. In an effort to divert Japan's interest from Korea and the Liaotung Peninsula, Russia let it be known to Japan, as early as December 1894, that there would be no interference in any Japanese plan to take Taiwan. Moreover, while Russian influence rose in Northeast Asia, British commercial interests were shifting from China to Japan.[41] There had been an unsuccessful movement, however, to form a British syndicate to purchase Taiwan from China.[42] Mercantile interests were seriously concerned that Japanese control of Taiwan would have unfavorable consequences for Great Britain.

One British naval commander even suggested that if Japan should obtain possession of Taiwan, Great Britain should then seize the Pescadores to insure the free passage of British trade in the Taiwan Strait.[43]

China, now, could no longer depend upon Great Britain to guarantee her territorial integrity, and the American position was too weak to turn the tide. Moreover, American interests were also shifting toward colonial expansion in the Pacific. In addition, France took an unrestrained interest in the Pescadores. The Co-operative Policy had finally come to a complete end, leaving Taiwan vulnerable to seizure. Consequently, when the Tripartite Intervention—comprising Russia, Germany, and France—sought the retrogression of the Liaotung Peninsula a week after the peace treaty was signed, Japan's possession of the island was given international guarantees.

The pattern established by this series of episodes clearly reveals that an international policy sympathetic to the maintenance of China's territorial integrity was operative each time that an external force posed a threat to the island in the latter half of the nineteenth century. Once that policy had disintegrated, as evidenced in the Sino-Japanese War, Taiwan became subject to foreign seizure. Another factor that can be discerned is that the Co-operative Policy among the major powers was frequently disturbed by internal disagreements within the various nations. Usually, this took the form of a conflict between the mercantile community in the port cities, often supported by military men and low ranking diplomatic officials, who wanted greater commercial opportunity and diplomatic privilege in China and their home governments, which preferred not to disturb China's viable growth and stable position in the international arena. While the agitation against the established policy of conciliation hindered its effectiveness, it had not, until the 1890s at least, overthrown it.

China, of course, welcomed the policy and attempted consciously to make use of it by citing the strength and strategy of her friends. It also encouraged China to make a genuine effort to promote a modernization program for Taiwan in the late 1880s. Unfortunately, it was not sustained and came too late to help in resisting Japan. In her resistance to territorial seizure, China was adamant and stood on her traditional claim to Chinese territory; namely, that sovereignty could never pass from China to another nation.[44] Her internal problems, however, coupled with external pressure and the lack of a sympathetic policy from any of the major powers, were responsible for the ultimate erosion in China's position on Taiwan.

Notes

1. For an excellent account of the career of Liu Ming-ch'uan, see Samuel Chu, "Liu Ming-ch'uan and Modernization of Taiwan," *The Journal of Asian Studies,* XXIII, 1 (November, 1963), 37-53.

2. Whereas the term Co-operative Policy, was either not specifically mentioned or was placed in quotation marks or lower case lettering, recent writers have been more bold. Masataka Banno in his *China and the West, 1858-1861: The Origins of the Tsungli Yamen* [(Cambridge, Mass., 1964), Harvard East Asian Series 15] identified it as follows: "In the 1860's the so-called Cooperative Policy was pursued by the major powers in Peking: Britain, the United States, France, and Russia cooperated with one another and with China" (pp. 243-44). Mary C. Wright in her *The Last Stand of Chinese Conservatism: The T'ung-Chih Restoration, 1862-1874* [(Stanford, 1957), Stanford Studies in History, Economics, and Political Science, XIII] has a chapter on the Co-operative Policy (Ch. III, pp. 21-42). While the concern of historians has been with the nature of this policy in the 1860s, it is the thesis of this paper that it was equally effective until 1895, and, indeed, had been given its most severe test—in the case of Taiwan, at least—*after* the 1860s.

3. For a summary, see H. B. Morse, *The International Relations of the Chinese Empire,* I: "The Period of Conflict, 1834-1860" (Shanghai, 1910), p. 293. See also reports to the western community in the *Chinese Repository,* XI, 627-29, 682-85; XII, 103-105, 113-21 (p. 114 contains a list of the casualties), 235-48, 500-503; XIV, 298-303. A vivid description of the difficulties encountered by the survivors can be found in: Great Britain, Public Record Office, Foreign Office Files [F.O.], series 17, Volume 59, no. 68, Henry Pottinger to the Earl of Aberdeen, despatch Dec. 4,

1842, and other letters in the same collection. The Chinese version can be found in *Ch'ing-tai ch'ou-pan i-wu-shih-mo* [IWSM], Tao Kuang [TK], *Chüan* 62, 15b-25b, 49b, 51b-52, 53; *Chüan* 63, 33; Supp. 1528-1538.

4. For a brief account of this and later episodes involving the United States, see Leonard Gordon, "Early American Relations with Formosa, 1849-1870," *The Historian,* XIX, 3 (May, 1957), 262-89.

5. Francis L. Hawks (ed.), *Narrative of the Expedition of an American Squadron to the China Seas and Japan, Performed in the Years 1852, 1853, and 1854, under the Command of Commodore M. C. Perry, United States Navy* (Washington, 1856) [published as *Sen. Exec. Doc.,* No. 79: 33rd Cong., 2nd Sess.], 3 vols., II, pp. 137-38, 143-45, 153-54, 156-63.

6. *Ibid.,* p. 178.

7. *Ibid.,* pp. 178-82. For a brief summary of Perry's concern with Taiwan, see *ibid.,* I, pp. 498-99.

8. William E. Griffis, *Townshend Harris: First American Envoy in Japan* (Boston, New York, 1895), p. 16. In a lengthy report to Secretary of State William L. Marcy, dated March 28, 1854, Harris proposed that Taiwan be purchased by the United States.

9. Documentation for this episode is fully discussed in correspondence published in U. S. Congress, *Senate Executive Documents,* No. 22: 35th Congress, 2nd Session, IX.

10. *Sen. Exec. Doc.,* No. 22: 35th Cong., 2nd Sess., IX, 1210-11. For Parker's proposal for joint action with the British and French, see pp. 1081-84.

11. *Ibid.,* pp. 1210-11.

12. *Ibid.,* pp. 1248-51.

13. William L. Marcy to Peter Parker, Feb. 27, 1857, National Archives, Records of the Dept. of State [RDS], Diplomatic Despatches [DD], China, Vol. 14.

14. William B. Reed to Lewis Cass, Dec. 28, 1857, RDS, DD, China, Vol. 15.

15. Nathan A. Pelcovits, *Old China Hands and the Foreign Office* (New York, 1948), pp. 15-17. The origins of

British policy changes are thoroughly discussed in this well-documented study. For a full account, see Introduction and Part I.

16. Pelcovits, *Old China Hands*, p. 21.

17. Official correspondence pertaining to this episode can be found in U. S. Department of State, *Diplomatic Correspondence*, 1867, pt. 1; RDS, DD, China, Vol. 24; RDS Consular Letters [CL], Amoy, Vol. 3.

18. Isaac J. Allen to William H. Seward, April 7, 1867, RDS, CL, Hong Kong, Vol. 6.

19. *Diplomatic Correspondence*, 1867, pt. 1, p. 498.

20. For a copy of the actual agreement between LeGendre and the aborigines' chieftain, see LeGendre to Seward, May 10, 1869, RDS, CL, Amoy, Vol. 4.

21. Great Britain, Parliament, House of Commons, *Sessional Papers*, "Correspondence Respecting the Attack on British Protestant Missionaries at Yang-chow-foo, August, 1868," China, No. 2 (1869), LXIV, p. 72.

22. *Ibid.*, "Correspondence Respecting Missionary Disturbances at Che-foo, and Taiwan (Formosa)," China, No. 3 (1869), LXIV, p. 105.

23. *Ibid.*, "Correspondence Respecting Outrage of British Merchants at Banca [Meng-chia] in Formosa," China, No. 6 (1869), LXIV, pp. 182-83.

24. *Ibid.*, "Correspondence Respecting Missionary Disturbances at Che-foo and Taiwan (Formosa)," China, No. 3 (1869), LXIV, pp. 110, 114-20, 138, 141-42, 151-52, 156-57.

25. *Ibid.*, pp. 125-26.

26. The account of these discussions and later diplomatic negotiations concerning Taiwan are recorded in Gaimushō [Ministry of foreign affairs] (GMS), *Nihon gaikō bunsho* [Japanese diplomatic documents] (NGB) (Tokyo, 1955–). VII (1874).

27. Watanabe Ikujirō et al. (comp.), *Ōkuma bunsho* [Ōkuma papers] (Tokyo, 1958–), I, pp. 17-26.

28. GMS, Gaikō shiryō [Diplomatic historical materials], Taiwan seitō jiken [The subjugation of Taiwan], MSS (bound

volume) in Ministry of Foreign Affairs, Japan Archives Section, Tokyo, secret, copy, pp. 167, 169.

29. Orders to Saigō Tsugumichi, dated March 3, 1874, Japanese Army, Navy Archives [JANA], Army Topic File [ATF], Taiwan Incident (1874-1875), Taiwan banchi jimu tori-shirabe no naimei sono-ta [Secret orders for investigation of the Taiwan aborigines land affairs, and others], First Bureau, Army Ministry, March 2-29, 1874, Taiwan shobun [The disposition of Taiwan], I (T1145). More laborers than soldiers had gone to Taiwan, and a considerable amount of construction equipment was also sent along.

30. The correspondence between the Chinese and Japanese diplomats on the Taiwan question was returned by both sides to their authors, as stipulated in the final agreement. They already formed enclosures to memorials to the Chinese emperor, however, and can be found in the IWSM, T'ung-chih [TC], *Chüan* 97, 37-65. The Japanese legation

at Peking kept stenographic notes on the conferences and later published them, along with any written memoranda that were exchanged (NGB, VII [1874], pp. 219-338).

31. NGB, VII (1874), pp. 225-26, 240-41, 258-60.

32. Notes on conversation between LeGendre and Wade, Oct. 9, 1874, and LeGendre to Ōkuma, Oct. 5, 1874, Ōkuma bunsho [Ōkuma papers], MSS, in Waseda Daigaku Tosho-kan [Waseda University Library], Tokyo (A4432).

33. NGB, VII (1874), pp. 277-92. Final negotiations are also described in IWSM, TC, Chüan 98, 11-17b. Wade's participation is described at length in his letter to the Minister of Foreign Affairs; see F.O. 405/16, no. 11, Thomas F. Wade to the Earl of Derby, Nov. 16, 1874.

34. For the French version of the Indo-Chinese conflict, see France, Ministère des affaires étrangères, *Documents Diplomatiques,* "Affaires du Tonkin, 1874-1883" (Paris, 1883), 2 vols., and "Affaires de Chine et du Tonkin, 1884-1885: L'Affaire du Tonkin, Histoire Diplomatique de l'établissement de notre conflict avec la Chine, 1882-1885" (Paris, n.d.); military activities in Taiwan and Foochow are discussed in Book II. The Chinese version, and the war itself,

is documented in Shao Hsun-cheng et al., eds., *Chung-fa chan-cheng* [The Sino-French War], Modern Chinese Historical Materials Series, No. 6 (Shanghai, 1955), 7 vols.; for events in Taiwan, see vol. V, pp. 562 *passim.*, VI.

35. For a discussion of this, see Pelcovits, *Old China Hands,* pp. 140, 146-47.

36. The arguments and counter-arguments in the controversial rice-contraband issue are recorded in: France, Ministère des affaires étrangères, *Documents Diplomatiques,* "Affaires de Chine, 1885-1899," (Paris, 1885-1901), pp. 17-22, 25-26, 30-32, 38 ff. *British Sessional Papers,* (1884-1885) LXXXVII, pp. 486 ff.

37. *Doc. Dipl.,* "Affaires de Chine et du Tonkin," pp. 19-21, 71-72.

38. For a brief account of this episode, see Leonard Gordon, "Japan's Interest in Taiwan, 1872-1895," *Orient/West,* 9/1 (January-February 1964), 54-56.

39. NGB (1895), XXVIII, Pt. 2, p. 398. This reference contains a full account of the pertinent documentation pertaining to this episode.

40. For a useful account of the Japanese military and diplomatic effort in the Sino-Japanese War, see Ino Yoshinori, *Taiwan bunka shi* (A gazetteer of Taiwan culture) (Tokyo, 1928), III.

41. Philip Joseph, *Foreign Diplomacy in China, 1894-1900* (London, 1928), p. 106. For an excellent account of British involvement in the negotiations, see F. Q. Quo, "British Diplomacy and the Cession of Formosa, 1894-1895," *Modern Asian Studies,* II, 2 (1968), 141-54.

42. F. O. 405/61, no. 440, N. R. O'Conor, British Minister at Peking, to the Earl of Kimberley, Dec. 21, 1894, F. O. 405/62, no. 187, O'Conor to the Earl of Kimberley, Jan. 19, 1895. Promoters were a London Syndicate under the auspices of the Jardine, Matheson, and Co.

43. F. O. 17/1252, Vice Adm. E. R. Freemantle to Secretary of the Admiralty, March 7, 1895.

44. Sophia Su-fei Yen in her *Taiwan in China's Foreign Relations, 1836-1874* (Hamden, Conn., 1965) places great

stress on this point as a deterrent to foreign aggrandizement against Taiwan and further asserts that it was the "jealousy" of the powers that prevented them from acquiring the island (see Part III and Conclusion). My view, as indicated by the thesis of this article, suggests the contrary as a more appropriate explanation. The Chinese received little satisfaction from their traditional claim, and the most significant aspects of the pattern of events concerning Taiwan is that the powers interceded.

PUBLICATIONS OF THE EAST ASIAN INSTITUTE

STUDIES

THE LADDER OF SUCCESS IN IMPERIAL CHINA by Ping-ti Ho. New York: Columbia University Press, 1962.

THE CHINESE INFLATION, 1937–1949 by Shun-hsin Chou. New York: Columbia University Press, 1963.

REFORMER IN MODERN CHINA: CHANG CHIEN, 1853–1926, by Samuel Chu. New York: Columbia University Press, 1965.

RESEARCH IN JAPANESE SOURCES: A GUIDE, by Herschel Webb with the assistance of Marleigh Ryan. New York: Columbia University Press, 1965.

SOCIETY AND EDUCATION IN JAPAN, by Herbert Passin. New York: Bureau of Publications, Teachers College, Columbia University, 1965.

AGRICULTURAL PRODUCTION AND ECONOMIC DEVELOPMENT IN JAPAN, 1873–1922, by James I. Nakamura. Princeton, N. J.: Princeton University Press, 1966.

JAPAN'S FIRST MODERN NOVEL: UKIGUMO OF FUTABATEI SHIMEI, by Marleigh Ryan. New York: Columbia University Press, 1967.

THE KOREAN COMMUNIST MOVEMENT: 1918–1948, by Dae-Sook Suh. Princeton, N. J.: Princeton University Press, 1967.

THE FIRST VIETNAM CRISIS, by Melvin Gurtov. New York: Columbia University Press, 1967.

Publications of the East Asian Institute

CADRES, BUREAUCRACY AND POLITICAL POWER IN COMMUNIST CHINA, by A. Doak Barnett. New York: Columbia University Press, 1967.

THE JAPANESE IMPERIAL INSTITUTION IN THE TOKUGAWA PERIOD, by Herschel Webb. New York: Columbia University Press, 1968.

THE RECRUITMENT OF UNIVERSITY GRADUATES IN BIG FIRMS IN JAPAN, by Koya Azumi. New York: Teachers College Press, Columbia University, 1968.

THE COMMUNISTS AND CHINESE PEASANT REBELLION: A STUDY IN THE REWRITING OF CHINESE HISTORY, by James P. Harrison, Jr., New York: Atheneum Publishers, 1969.

HOW THE CONSERVATIVES RULE JAPAN, by Nathaniel B. Thayer. Princeton, N. J.: Princeton University Press, 1969.

ASPECTS OF CHINESE EDUCATION, edited by C. T. Hu. New York: Teachers College Press, Columbia University, 1969.

IMPERIAL RESTORATION IN MEDIEVAL JAPAN, by Paul Varley. New York: Columbia University Press (forthcoming).

ECONOMIC DEVELOPMENT AND THE LABOR MARKET IN JAPAN, by Koji Taira. New York: Columbia University Press (forthcoming).

LI TSUNG-JEN, A Memoir. Edited by T. K. Tong. University of California Press (forthcoming).

DOCUMENTS ON KOREAN COMMUNISM, by Dae-Sook Suh. Princeton, N. J.: Princeton University Press (forthcoming).

THE JAPANESE OLIGARCHY AND THE RUSSO-JAPANESE WAR, by Shumpei Okamoto. New York: Columbia University Press (forthcoming).

Publications of the East Asian Institute

REPRINTS

THE COMMUNIST MOVEMENT IN CHINA, by Ch'en Kung-po, edited with an introduction by C. Martin Wilbur. New York: Octagon Books, 1966.

AMERICAN POLICY AND THE CHINESE REVOLUTION, 1925–1928, by Dorothy Borg. New York: Octagon Books, 1968.

THE FABRIC OF CHINESE SOCIETY, by Morton H. Fried. New York: Octagon Books (forthcoming).

RESEARCH AIDS

SINO-JAPANESE RELATIONS, 1862–1927: A CHECKLIST OF THE CHINESE FOREIGN MINISTRY ARCHIVES, compiled by Kuo Ting-yee and edited by James W. Morley. New York: East Asian Institute, 1965.

CHINESE LAW PAST AND PRESENT: A BIBLIOGRAPHY OF ENACTMENTS AND COMMENTARIES IN ENGLISH TEXT, compiled and edited by Fu-shun Lin. New York: East Asian Institute, 1966.

THE RESEARCH ACTIVITIES OF THE SOUTH MANCHURIAN RAILWAY COMPANY, 1907–45: A HISTORY AND BIBLIOGRAPHY, by John Young. New York: East Asian Institute, 1966.

THE DISTRIBUTION OF FAMILY NAMES IN TAIWAN, VOLUME I: THE DATA, by Chen Shao-hsing and Morton H. Fried. Taipei, Taiwan: Chinese Materials and Research Aids Service Center, Inc., 1969.

JAPANESE SOCIETY: A BIBLIOGRAPHY OF MATERIALS IN THE ENGLISH LANGUAGE, compiled and edited by Herbert Passin. New York: East Asian Institute (forthcoming).

Publications of the East Asian Institute

OCCASIONAL PAPERS

HISTORIANS AND AMERICAN FAR EASTERN POLICY, compiled by Dorothy Borg. New York, East Asian Institute, 1966.

AMERICAN PRESURRENDER PLANNING FOR POST-WAR JAPAN by Hugh Borton. New York, East Asian Institute, 1967.

IMPERIAL JAPAN AND ASIA: A REASSESSMENT, compiled by Grant K. Goodman. New York, East Asian Institute, 1967.

REALITY AND ILLUSION: THE HIDDEN CRISIS BETWEEN JAPAN AND THE U.S.S.R., 1932–1934 by Ikuhiko Hata. New York, East Asian Institute, 1967.

PROVINCIAL PARTY PERSONNEL IN MAINLAND CHINA, 1956–1966 by Frederick C. Teiwes. New York, East Asian Institute, 1967.

THE LEGACY OF THE OCCUPATION–JAPAN by Herbert Passin. New York, East Asian Institute, 1968.

TAIWAN: STUDIES IN CHINESE LOCAL HISTORY, edited by Leonard H. D. Gordon. Columbia University Press, 1970.

Index

Index

Index

Index